Uncle John's
iFlush
Hunting for Heroes

BATHROOM READER FOR KIDS ONLY!

by
Patrick
Merrell

. . . .

Bathroom Readers' Press
Ashland, Oregon

UNCLE JOHN'S IFLUSH: HUNTING FOR HEROES
BATHROOM READER® FOR KIDS ONLY

For information, write:
The Bathroom Readers' Institute
P.O. Box 1117
Ashland, OR 97520
www.bathroomreader.com

Illustration and book design by Patrick Merrell
www.patrickmerrell.com
Dedicated to the Mount Vernon Public Library

ISBN-10: 1-62686-041-6 / ISBN-13: 978-1-62686-041-4
Library of Congress Cataloging-in-Publication Data
Uncle John's iflush hunting for heroes bathroom reader for kids only!
    pages cm
ISBN 978-1-62686-041-4 (hardback)
1. Wit and humor, Juvenile. 2. Curiosities and wonders—Juvenile
literature. I. Bathroom Readers' Institute (Ashland, Or.)
II. Title: iFlush hunting for heroes bathroom reader for kids only.
PN6166.U535 2014
818'.60208—dc23

2013036654

Printed in the United States of America
First Printing: May, 2014

18 17 16 15 14   6 5 4 3 2 1

. . . .

Thanks: A hearty high-four (sorry, that's all the fingers
I have) to some humans who helped make this book possible:

Gordon Javna	Jay Newman	Blake Mitchum	Matthew Lighty
Kim T. Griswell	Trina Janssen	Carly Stephenson	Brandon Walker
Brian Boone	Aaron Guzman	Joan Kyzer	Thomas Crapper

iOpener
Greetings

What is a hero? To some people, it's a long sandwich made with bologna and mayo and, if they're really lucky, cheese. *You* might call that a submarine or grinder or hoagie, but it doesn't really matter because that's not the kind of hero we're talking about.

The pages that follow are filled with heroes who have saved the day, sacrificed themselves for others, or inspired us with their accomplishments—great, small, or just plain goofy:

- **At the Airport:** Fearsome Falcons on Patrol
- **Civil War:** Women Spies…for the North and South
- **In the Classroom:** Brooklyn's Unlikely Chess Whizzes
- **Armenia:** Finswimming Champ to the Rescue
- **Around the World:** Five Amazing Super-Rodents
- **Africa:** Two Kids Changing the World, plus
- **A 100-year-old Marathoner in a Turban**

So, whenever you're ready, go to the…

Intro on page 6

And we're off and flushing!

Contents

Bathroom user...

… prepare to dive into the greatest **toilet-themed adventure** ever devised by a group of **mad-scientist-type plumbers** and hosted by a bedraggled-yet-charming **lab rat** named **Dwayne**. That's me.

But, first, a quick explanation.

Copying how **computers** have been connected together to form the **Internet**, a top-secret plumbing team known as the **Four P's** linked the world's **sewer lines** together to create the **Interpipe**. You probably think I'm making that up, but this book is based on how it actually works!

The Four P's

Plumb Bob · Phyllis Tanks · P. Liddy · Portia Potty

Flush yourself down a toilet in **Walla Walla** (that's a city in the northwest part of the United States) and next thing you know, you're in **Katmandu** (that's, like, all the way on the other side of the world).

Wait, it gets even better!

The Four P's also created a waterproof device called the **iSwirl** that can be used to travel back in time, spinning through the years in a mere flush of the toilet! Is that not totally cool… and wet?

Yeah, I thought you'd agree.

So here's how this is going to work.

I'm gonna flush myself down this toilet, and you're gonna follow along. I'll be visiting a **different place** and a **different year** every time you turn the page. Solve the **puzzle** you find there, and you can move on—in one of three ways.

1. Follow the **pipes** to the next page; **2.** jump to the page shown on the **iSwirl** (in the lower right-hand corner) to travel through the book in order from the earliest date to the most recent; or **3.** visit pages any old way you want!

Sound like a plan?

Then let's get going! I'll jump in, you turn the page, and away we GO!

Note:

If you want to keep your book clean, use a separate piece of paper (toilet paper not recommended!) for solving the puzzles.

Go to the page shown.

1918

Where: Verdun, France, during World War I. About 200 U.S. soldiers are under fire from the enemy…and their own side!

Air Mail

Hup Two Three Four

Yikes! It's noisy, dangerous, and mucky here. Luckily, a **pigeon** named **Cher Ami** is about to single-footedly save the day.

On October 2, more than 500 men from the U.S. First Army's **77th Division** charged into the **Argonne Forest**. They soon found themselves trapped in an overgrown ravine, surrounded by Germans. Back at headquarters, nobody knew where they were—or if they were even alive.

Food and ammunition started running low, and the soldiers had to crawl to a nearby stream, bullets whizzing over their heads, to get water. Their only means of communication: three homing pigeons.

BANG

One of the soldiers attached a note to the first pigeon's leg and released it. The Germans shot it down. The same thing happened to the second pigeon. Then, artillery shells started exploding all around the Americans. It came from their own side, miles away. Friendly fire!

Their last hope: a pigeon named Cher Ami. Unfortunately, as the bird flew skyward, bullets struck him in the chest and leg. He landed with a thud on the ground. But then something amazing happened. Despite his wounds, Cher Ami got up, spread his wings, and completed the 25-mile flight back to headquarters.

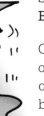

Soon after, reinforcements fought their way to the **Lost Battalion**, the name given the group of surviving soldiers.

Cher Ami lost his right leg, but doctors patched up the rest of him. The French awarded him the **Croix de Guerre** ("war cross"), a medal given to foreign soldiers for heroic deeds in battle. After his death, his one-legged body went on display at the **National Museum of American History** in Washington, D.C.

Radios were used during World War I, but each one required 3 or 4 mules to carry all the equipment. …

iPuzzle
Pigeon Towed

At right is the message Cher Ami carried, saving the lives of 200 soldiers. Which route should he follow to bring it to headquarters?

We are along the road parallel to 276.4. Our own artillery is dropping a barrage directly on us. For heaven's sake, stop it.

Critter Medals: During World War II, the United Kingdom awarded the Dickin Medal to animals that helped in the effort. Among the winners: 32 pigeons, 18 dogs, 3 horses, and 1 cat. Simon, the cat, won partly for getting rid of rats aboard a British ship, the HMS *Amethyst*. Hmmph!

Year: 1925
Page: 30

Jump to this page **or** follow the pipes.

2002

Where: Jolly old Cornwall, England, with a milkman who's the cream of the crop.

Milkman to the Rescue

Mild-mannered **milkman** Steve Leech, 35, was on his usual rounds delivering milk in southwestern **England**. But, as he passed by a gift shop, he noticed clouds of smoke coming out of it.

"I saw the flats [apartments] up above and thought I'd better do something," he said. Leech called the fire department but didn't wait for them to arrive. "I kicked the door in and started pouring milk everywhere."

It took 320 pints of milk, but by the time the **firefighters** arrived 10 minutes later, Leech had mostly put out the blaze. The pros finished the job but credited him with helping to save the lives of eight people who lived above the shop.

"It was hard work opening all those bottles, especially since they have tamperproof lids," Leech said. He then jokingly added, "But it was even harder trying to explain to my boss where all the milk had gone."

A year later, the **National Dairymen's Association** named Leech "Hero Milkman of the Millennium." (That's 1,000 years!)

— — — —

Hose Hero

In 2011 in Northern Ireland, Michael Coyle saved the day using a tanker truck filled with milk. A car had crashed and burst into flames along his route. Two badly injured men were pinned inside. Coyle quickly backed his tanker up to the car, pulled out a hose, and sprayed the raging fire with milk, saving both men.

Move one "E" in LEECH to the end, and it spells LECHE, the Spanish word for "milk."

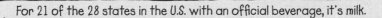

iPuzzle
Milk Made

Use the clues to fill in the blank spaces. Then transfer the letters to the same-numbered boxes below. *Ta-da*! You've got the answers to two jokes.

A. The sound a pig makes: ____ ____ ____ ____
$\qquad\qquad\qquad\quad$ 18 $\quad$ 6 $\quad$ 19 $\quad$ 13

B. Sick: ____ ____ ____
$\qquad\quad$ 11 $\quad$ 3 $\quad$ 7

C. The month before April: ____ ____ ____ ____ ____
$\qquad\qquad\qquad\qquad\quad$ 5 $\quad$ 9 $\quad$ 16 $\quad$ 14 $\quad$ 1

D. Body of water bigger than a pond: ____ ____ ____ ____
$\qquad\qquad\qquad\qquad\qquad\quad$ 12 $\quad$ 15 $\quad$ 8 $\quad$ 4

E. A male turkey (or a boy's name): ____ ____ ____
$\qquad\qquad\qquad\qquad\qquad\quad$ 17 $\quad$ 2 $\quad$ 10

What kind of milk is used to make Swiss cheese?

1	2	3	4	■	5	6	7	8

What contains milk but can't be eaten or drunk?

9	■	10	11	12	13	■	14	15	16	17	18	19

- - - - - - - - - - PROJECT - - - - - - - - - -

Milk Dice: Have an adult heat up one cup of milk (not boiling). Mix in one tablespoon of white vinegar and stir the mixture until lumps form. Strain off all the liquid, then mold the lumps together into four small cubes. Let the cubes dry (they'll become rock hard after a few days). Paint black dots on the cubes to make dice. Now you've got something to use for the game on page 13!

Jump to this page **or** follow the pipes.

1976

Where: Armenia, when it was part of the Soviet Union. It's now a country all by itself.

Dive, Dive, Dive!

Champion swimmer **Shavarsh Karapetyan** usually dives into the water wearing a dolphin-like tail on his feet. Why? He's a **finswimmer**, and one of the best. He's set 11 world records and won more championships than you can shake a snorkel at.

Shavarsh Karapetyan

But today he's about to accomplish his greatest swimming feat—minus the dolphin tail. A **bus** traveling on a road above **Yerevan Lake** has just veered out of control and plunged into the icy water. Trapped inside: 92 passengers. Karapetyan and his brother (both had just finished a training run) raced to the rescue.

Both feet slip into a finswimmer's "tail," called a monofin.

Karapetyan dove down to the bus, 33 feet (10 m) below. He broke the rear window and swam in, cutting his back and legs on the jagged glass. One by one, he pulled people to the surface. "It was so dark down there that I could barely see anything. One of my dives, I accidentally grabbed a seat instead of a passenger," he said.

He made 30 dives, each lasting about half a minute, while his brother hauled survivors to shore. Karapetyan then collapsed, unconscious from the effort. He remained that way for a month and a half in the hospital.

When he finally came to, his body had been so damaged by the cold water and the sewage in it that he could no longer compete as a finswimmer. But there was a reward: 20 of the bus's passengers lived, thanks to Shavarsh Karapetyan.

But Wait, There's More

In 1985, Shavarsh Karapetyan saw a burning building and rushed in. He suffered severe burns while saving the people trapped inside, resulting in another long hospital stay.

Finswimmers travel through the water about twice as fast as regular swimmers.

iPuzzle
Swim Meet

A game to play with friends, or against Dwayne, using one die.

Pick a lane. If you're swimming alone, pick another lane for Dwayne,
your competition. Take turns rolling the die (you roll for Dwayne).
If the roll is a 1, cross off the S in your lane. If it's a 2, cross off the W,
and so on (you'll need two 4's and two 5's). Only the rolling player crosses
off a letter. The first player to finish their SWIM MEET is the champ.

S 1	S 1	S 1	S 1	S 1	S 1
W 2	W 2	W 2	W 2	W 2	W 2
I 3	I 3	I 3	I 3	I 3	I 3
M 4	M 4	M 4	M 4	M 4	M 4
M 4	M 4	M 4	M 4	M 4	M 4
E 5	E 5	E 5	E 5	E 5	E 5
E 5	E 5	E 5	E 5	E 5	E 5
T 6	T 6	T 6	T 6	T 6	T 6

Make your
own die on
page 11.

Draw the
lanes on a
separate
piece of
paper if you
want.

Year: 1980
Page: 32

Jump to this
page **or** follow
the pipes.

Some finswimmers use a separate swimfin on each foot.

Some finswimmers pop up to breathe. In other finswimming events, snorkels or air tanks are used.

1942

Where: The United States, then continuing on to England, India, Italy, and finally Japan.

Rodent Power

A fashion show of the outfits these super-rodents wear.

Here's my Fave Five list of the finest, funnest, fittest **rodent superheroes** the world has ever seen.

Mighty Mouse (U.S. movie shorts, 1942): The granddaddy of super-rodents, **Mighty Mouse** hit it big in 1955 when he moved from movie theaters to television. In an early episode, he got his power from eating vitamins A, B, C, D, E, and XYZ.

Danger Mouse (British TV, 1981): A secret-agent superhero who wears a black eyepatch and an all-white suit. To save money, the artists often drew him in pitch-black rooms, where only his one eye showed, or in all-white scenes at the **North Pole**. He's assisted by another rodent, **Penfold**, a cowardly hamster who cries "Crumbs, DM!" when things go wrong.

Dinkan (Indian kid's magazine, *Balamangalam*, 1983): When he was young, Dinkan was captured by **aliens** and taken to their home planet. Experiments performed on Dinkan made him extra strong, with powerful senses and the ability to fly.

Rat-Man (Italian comic book, 1989): Imitating **Batman**, Rat-man has a Ratmobile, Rat-Cave, and a sidekick named Tòpin the Wonder Mouse. Rat-Man was known as Rat-Boy and MarvelMouse in his early days and Zappo the Embarrassing Man during one story where he lost his memory.

Pikachu (Japanese video game, *Pokémon Red and Blue*, 1996): A chubby mouselike critter with red cheeks that store electricity. Pikachu has also appeared on trading cards and in the **Macy's Thanksgiving Day Parade**. *Time* magazine ranked him second on their "Best People of 1999" list, two places ahead of Harry Potter's creator, **J.K. Rowling**. He's not a "people," but I guess there are worse insults.

Create your own rat superhero on the last page of this book.

iPuzzle
Rodent Chase

"Catch" each rodent on the list by circling it in the grid.
Look for them reading forward, backward, up, down, or diagonally.

BEAVER
CAPYBARA
CHINCHILLA
CHIPMUNK
GERBIL
GOPHER
GROUNDHOG
GUINEA PIG
HAMSTER
JERBOA
LEMMING
MARMOT
MOUSE
PORCUPINE
SQUIRREL
VOLE
WOODCHUCK

```
M G C H I N C H I L L A
O X B T A Y A D Y D P R
G L B O G M O N R A O A
R I I M O U S E S V R B
O B P R P X V T D X C Y
U R X A H A J Y E V U P
N E K M E E X P K R P A
D G J B R N A X S Z I C
H V V B C H I P M U N K
O W O O D C H U C K E X
G A L E M M I N G X X X
U L E R R I U Q S R O K
```

It's Fat Rink!

Er... Frat Ink!

I mean Rat Fink!

Rat Fink: Although not a superhero, an honorable mention goes to Rat Fink. Created by Ed "Big Daddy" Roth in the late '50s, Rat Fink is green with a big mouth, pointy little teeth, and bulging, bloodshot eyes. Shown here: a '60s Rat Fink ring.

Year: 1944
Page: 74
Go Return

Jump to this page **or** follow the pipes.

1992 — **Where:** In a carpet factory near Lahore, Pakistan, where kids slave away in factories. But one of them has had enough!

A Rug-ged Life

Compared to his size, 10-year-old **Iqbal Masih** has got to be one of the biggest heroes ever. He weighs only 60 pounds (27 kg), but most of that is grit, hope, and bravery.

Iqbal Masih

In 1986, when Iqbal was four years old, his mother needed money for her family. A **carpet factory** owner loaned her 600 rupees ($12). In exchange, Iqbal had to work for the man until the loan was repaid.

These loans, called *peshgi*, are very hard to repay. Iqbal earned no money during his first year of training. On top of that, the carpet man charged for the food Iqbal ate and the tools he used. And whenever Iqbal made a mistake, more money was added to the debt. After six years of work, and some additional loans, Iqbal's mother owed much, much more.

Iqbal and the other children alongside him worked in bad conditions. They crouched on benches, sometimes in the broiling heat, for 14 hours a day, six days a week, tying knots to make carpets.

In 1992, Iqbal found a way out. He attended a meeting of the **BLLF** (Bonded Labor Liberation Front) and learned that Pakistan's **National Assembly** had just outlawed the kind of work he was doing, known as **bonded labor**.

The BLLF helped him gain his freedom, but Iqbal didn't stop there. He worked hard to free other kids, even sneaking into factories to get more information. He gave speeches to publicize what was going on and traveled to other countries to talk at schools.

Iqbal was shot and killed in 1995, short of his thirteenth birthday. Some people think the carpet factory owners arranged it to keep him quiet. There's no proof of that, but if they did, it didn't work. Iqbal's memory lives on, inspiring others to continue the battle against bonded labor.

iPuzzle
Iqbal Masih

The words below are spelled using the letters in IQBAL MASIH. Working off the words we've written in, there's only one way to fit the rest into each puzzle. Counting the number of letters will help you.

HI	LAB	~~LAMB~~	SHAM
AIL	BALM	LASH	ALIBI
AIM	~~BASH~~	LIMB	BASIL
HAS	BIAS	MASH	SALAMI

← These words go in this puzzle.

These words go in this puzzle. ⟶

~~AS~~	ALAS	MAIL	SLAM
AHA	BAIL	SAIL	~~SLIM~~
ASH	HAIL	SHIM	ALIAS
~~HIS~~	IBIS	SLAB	BALSAM

Why Kids? Carpet-factory owners value children's tiny fingers, which can make the small, tight knots needed for high-quality carpets. It's estimated that about a million kids under the age of 14 work in these factories, mostly in Asia. For some kids, it's an accepted part of life, a way to earn a bit of money to help their struggling families.

Year: 1992
Page: 40
Go Return

Jump to this page **or** follow the pipes.

1967　**Where:** On the set of *Star Trek,* a TV show that takes place in the 23rd century but is making history right here in the 20th.

Space Race

Nichols as Lieutenant Uhura

At the end of **Star Trek**'s first season, African-American actress **Nichelle Nichols** decided she'd had enough of playing **Lieutenant Uhura**, the ship's communications officer. She wanted to sing in Broadway musicals. The show's creator, **Gene Roddenberry**, didn't want her to leave and asked her to take the weekend to reconsider.

The next day Roddenberry got some help from an unexpected source. Nichols was speaking at a fundraiser for the **NAACP** (National Association for the Advancement of Colored People). When told a big fan wanted to meet her, she expected some pimply, space-crazed kid. It turned out to be the country's leading voice for African-American rights—**Martin Luther King, Jr.**!

Her No. 1 fan

"He told me that I was one of the most important people in his family," Nichols said. "That they watched *Star Trek* and that I was a role model and their hero." Speechless at first, she thanked Dr. King, then told him she'd just decided to leave the show.

"STOP! You cannot!" King responded. "This is not a female role. This is not a black role. This is a quality role, and this is an equal role, and it is in a command position." In those days, African Americans rarely appeared on TV, mostly in small roles as maids or nannies. He added, "For the first time, the world sees us as we should be seen, as intelligent, beautiful, qualified people just like anyone else….This is what we're fighting for."

How could she say no to that! On Monday, when Nichols told Roddenberry about her talk with Dr. King and that she'd decided to stay on the show, a tear rolled down his cheek. She continued to play Uhura throughout the series three-year run and then in six *Star Trek* movies.

iPuzzle
Partner-Ship

Star Trek took place aboard the U.S.S. *Enterprise*.
Which two *Enterprise* ships below are exactly the same?

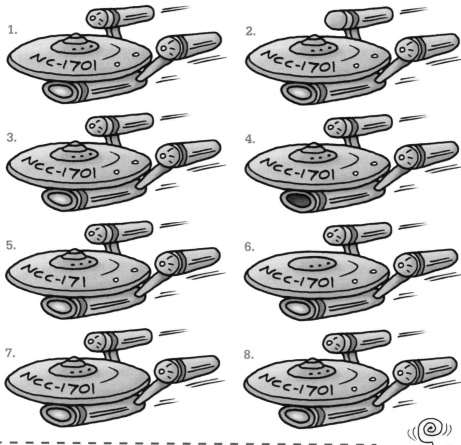

1. NCC-1701
2. Ncc-1701
3. Ncc-1701
4. Ncc-1701
5. Ncc-171
6. Ncc-1701
7. Ncc-1701
8. Ncc-1701

NASA Recruiter: In the 1970s and 1980s, Nichelle Nichols worked with NASA to recruit women and minorities. Among those she helped bring into the program were Sally Ride, the first American woman in space, and Guion Bluford, the first African-American astronaut.

Year: 1973
Page: 78
Go Return

Jump to this page **or** follow the pipes.

STAR spelled backward is RATS.

2004

Where: Woodville, New Zealand, in the middle of a raging storm, a morning fit for neither farmer nor beast.

Udder Success

Crikey! This is no time to be in a drainpipe. There's water everywhere—turning roads into rivers, washing away bridges, filling living rooms, and pelting down from the sky by the bucketful.

As the storm raged, dairy farmer **Kim Riley** had just one concern: getting her 350 cows to safety. But when she tried to herd them to dry ground, the churning floodwater whisked her and part of the herd away. Riley grabbed at trees and a fence, but the current was too strong. At one point, several of the cows swam over her head, forcing her down. "I drank a fair bit of water," she said.

Worst of all, the **Manawatu River Gorge**, with its dangerous rock walls, loomed ahead. "I thought if I was washed into the main river I would be gone," she said. But then, as hope seemed to drain away, a rescuer approached.

"I looked back and saw one of the last cows bearing down on me. As she went by I threw my arm over her neck." The black-and-white cow didn't even have a name, just a number—569.

Riley joked later about Cow 569, "She didn't say, 'Ooh, there's the boss. I better go and get her.' She's a bit of a stroppy old tart, and she would've probably thought, 'Get off me, you lug.'" Cow 569 got them both to shore, where they sat puffing and shaking from their 30-minute swim. Riley said, "She didn't set out to be a hero, but she definitely did save me."

Three years later, Riley retired Cow 569. "Most retired dairy cows become hamburgers, but not that one," she said. Cow 569 still had no name, but she did sport a new tag on one ear. It read "life saver."

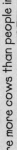

There are more cows than people in New Zealand.

The 2004 New Zealand flood was the worst on the North Island in over 100 years.

iPuzzle

Cowabunga

Match up each joke with the correct punch line.

1. ___ Why are cow barns noisy?

2. ___ What did the lazy cattle rancher say about his work?

3. ___ What stands in the field and says "mmmmm"?

4. ___ How do you make a milkshake?

5. ___ Where do cows eat lunch?

6. ___ What happens when you talk to a cow?

7. ___ Where do you go to see ancient cows?

8. ___ What is the most common cow illness?

9. ___ What happened to the fly when it flew into the bull's face?

10. ___ What does an upside-down cow say?

A. It hit the bull's-eye.

B. The calf-eteria.

C. They're filled with horns.

D. OOOW (look at it upside down)

E. I never herd.

F. A cow whose lips are stuck together.

G. Give a cow a pogo stick.

H. The mooseum.

I. It goes in one ear and out the udder.

J. Hay fever.

Cows Float: Many people don't realize it, but cows don't sink in water. The process of digesting grass creates methane gas, which is lighter than air. The cows' stomachs usually contain enough methane to keep them afloat.

Year: 2004
Page: 50

Jump to this page **or** follow the pipes.

1777

Where: Fredericksburg, New York (later known as Kent) during the American Revolution.

The Midnight Ride of Sybil Ludington

On April 26, two thousand **British troops** marched into the unprotected town of **Danbury, Connecticut**. They burned buildings, attacked innocent people, and destroyed supplies intended for colonial forces.

A messenger galloped off to alert **Colonel Henry Ludington**, commander of the only American troops in the area. He found the colonel at home, but his soldiers were all on leave, scattered around the countryside planting their spring crops.

The colonel needed to gather his men quickly, but how? The messenger could go no further, and Colonel Ludington had to stay where he was to organize things when his soldiers arrived.

The colonel's 16-year-old daughter, **Sybil**, stepped forward. She could ride as well as anyone, plus she knew the area and her father's men. It wouldn't be easy—rain, cold, a moonless night, rough roads, and outlaws in the woods known as "skinners" awaited. But that didn't stop Sybil.

She hopped on **Star**, her horse, and rode through the cold, dark night banging on doors with a long stick. When she arrived back home after her 40-mile (65 km) ride, shivering, drenched, and exhausted, almost all of her father's 421 men had been rallied. Led by Colonel Ludington, the men marched on Danbury and chased the British soldiers back to their ships in **Long Island Sound**.

Later, **George Washington**, impressed by Sybil's bravery, personally thanked her.

Giddy up!

← A sign in Mahopac Falls, the southernmost point of Sybil's ride

NEW YORK

SYBIL LUDINGTON
RODE HORSEBACK OVER THIS ROAD THE NIGHT OF APRIL 26, 1777, TO CALL OUT COLONEL LUDINGTON'S REGIMENT TO REPEL BRITISH AT DANBURY. CONN.
STATE EDUCATION DEPARTMENT. 1935

Paul Revere's famous ride in 1775 was only half as long as Sybil Ludington's.

iPuzzle
Trail Mix

We've scrambled up the names of 10 places on this map of Sybil Ludington's route. Each is an anagram (all the same letters in a different order) of one of the actual names listed on the left.

The actual names:

A. FARMERS MILLS

B. CRANE'S TAVERN

C. KENT CLIFFS

D. LAKE CARMEL

E. LAKE GLENEIDA

F. MAHOPAC MINES

G. PECKSVILLE

H. REDDING CORNERS

I. STORMVILLE

J. WHITE POND

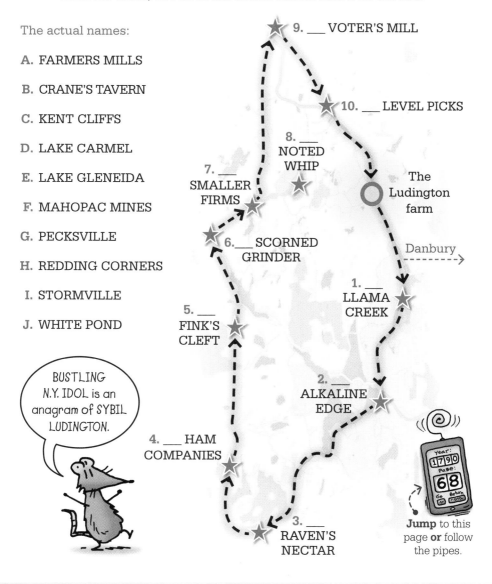

9. ___ VOTER'S MILL

10. ___ LEVEL PICKS

8. ___ NOTED WHIP

7. ___ SMALLER FIRMS

The Ludington farm

6. ___ SCORNED GRINDER

Danbury

1. ___ LLAMA CREEK

5. ___ FINK'S CLEFT

2. ___ ALKALINE EDGE

BUSTLING N.Y. IDOL is an anagram of SYBIL LUDINGTON.

4. ___ HAM COMPANIES

3. ___ RAVEN'S NECTAR

Year: 1790
Page: 68
Go   Return

Jump to this page **or** follow the pipes.

1902

Where: The Bureau of Chemistry's basement dining hall in Washington, D.C., where a dozen men are eating…poison!

We're Dying to Try It

People think rats will eat anything, but I'm steering clear of what's being dished up here. In between courses of soup, roast turkey, and rice pudding, the chef is serving capsules of **borax**, a bitter white powder used in detergents and fertilizers.

Why? It's part of a plan by the U.S. government to test the safety of common **food additives**. Twelve men have agreed to eat all their meals here— and to not sue if they get sick or die! Surprisingly, there's been no problem getting enough healthy young volunteers, most of them already government workers, for what the press calls the **Poison Squad**.

The Poison Squad's first "table trials" included borax, one of the most common food preservatives at the time. How did it go? Not good. As the borax doses increased, the men suffered appetite loss, headaches, and stomachaches.

Other food additives, such as **formaldehyde** and **copper sulfate**, did much worse. They caused liver, brain, and kidney damage. They also caused a big increase in visits to the toilet by the Poison Squad…for every reason you can imagine, but try not to. :-(

The mastermind behind the project, **Dr. Harvey Wiley**, kept detailed records. He constantly weighed the men, took their temperatures and pulses, and wrote down exactly what they ate. He then made his findings public. The result: In 1906 Congress passed the country's first two laws to regulate food, the **Pure Food and Drug Act** and the **Meat Inspection Act**.

So next time you eat something and don't get sick, give a wave of your napkin to the brave stomachs of the Poison Squad.

One Poison Squad member, William O. Robinson, lived to the age of 94.

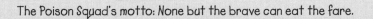

The Poison Squad's motto: None but the brave can eat the fare.

iPuzzle
Soup-Doku

soup bowl ⌄   borax **B**

mug   fork

Draw in the missing pictures
following the rules in the example.

All 4 pictures in each column ⟶

All 4 ⟶ pictures in each row

All 4 ⟶ pictures in each bold box

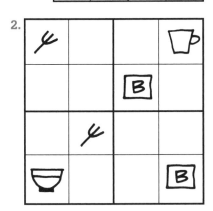

1.

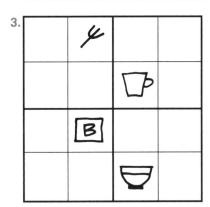

2.

3.

Blecch, Borax! At the beginning of Dr. Wiley's table trials, borax was mixed into the butter. But it tasted bitter, so the Poison Squad members stopped eating it. Same thing when borax was hidden in milk, meat, or coffee. So Dr. Wiley just put it in gelatin-coated capsules that the diners could swallow without tasting the stuff.

Year: 1907
Page: 66

Jump to this page **or** follow the pipes.

1057

Where: Kaifeng, China, in the courtroom of a judge with a crescent-moon scar on his forehead.

Bao, Wow!

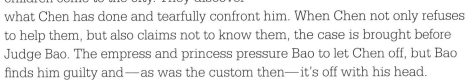

No one messes with **Judge Bao Zheng**, a fearless force of fairness in Chinese operas, books, and hit TV shows for 500 years.

In one tale, a man named **Chen Shimei** comes to the capital city to take the **imperial exam**. After getting the highest score, he hides the fact that he has a wife and two children, and weds the emperor's daughter. Three years later, his starving wife and children come to the city. They discover what Chen has done and tearfully confront him. When Chen not only refuses to help them, but also claims not to know them, the case is brought before Judge Bao. The empress and princess pressure Bao to let Chen off, but Bao finds him guilty and—as was the custom then—it's off with his head.

Bao Now

BAO GOING
GOING GONG

Here comp
da Judge

Bao

The inspiration for Bao Zheng? A real judge of the same name. The real Judge Bao never faced that case, but the story captures everything he stood for. Having grown up among working people, he understood their struggles. As a judge, he changed the system so that common people could present their complaints directly to city officials. Before that, clerks often took bribes from the rich and powerful to make cases go away. He also ruled against important officials more than 30 times, including men close to the emperor.

Other judges might be punished or fired for rulings like that, but not Bao. He was so respected, Emperor Renzong (in power at the time) promoted him. Even today, Chinese judges look to Judge Bao as an example of complete honesty and fairness for all.

iPuzzle
Take a Bao

Find one run of four blue characters in a row and one run of four green characters. Each foursome runs either straight across, down, or diagonally.

包拯 ← Bao Zheng's name in Chinese

包 拯 拯 包 包 拯 拯 拯 包 包 包 拯 拯
包 拯 包 拯 包 拯 包 拯 包 拯 包 包 包
包 包 包 拯 拯 包 包 包 拯 拯 包 拯 拯
拯 包 包 包 拯 包 拯 拯 拯 包 包 拯 拯
包 拯 拯 拯 包 包 包 拯 拯 拯 包 包 包
包 包 拯 拯 包 拯 拯 拯 包 包 包 拯 包
拯 包 包 包 拯 包 包 拯 拯 包 包 拯
包 包 拯 拯 包 包 拯 拯 包 拯 拯 拯 包
包 拯 包 包 拯 包 包 拯 包 拯 拯 包 包
包 拯 拯 拯 包 包 拯 包 包 包 拯 包 包

Tomb It May Concern: Millions of people visit the tomb of Bao Zheng as well as a nearby park and temple built in his honor. Recently, a wax museum with a life-size statue of Judge Bao was also added. Judge Bao fans can even buy T-shirts with his face on them at the gift shop.

Year: 1777
Page: 22

Jump to this page **or** follow the pipes.

1863

Where: America during the Civil War, where a battle is taking place ... to gain information.

Secret Agents *ladies*

Spies come in all shapes and sizes. During the **Civil War**, that included women who snooped and duped to get the scoop.

NORTHERN SPIES

Harriet the Spy: **Harriet Tubman** is most famous as a "conductor" on the **Underground Railroad**, helping transport slaves to freedom. But she was also the ringleader of a wartime spy network made up of former slaves. In 1863 she even helped lead a raid up the **Combahee River** in South Carolina to free 700 slaves.

Role-Playing: **Pauline Cushman**, a stage actress, gained the trust of the South one night when she proposed a toast to the **Confederacy** on stage. It was all an act. Soon, Southern officers were sharing secrets with her, which she passed on to the North.

Dashing Damsel: **Belle Boyd**, a 17-year-old Southern lass, picked up valuable information by mingling with Northern troops that occupied her hometown in **Virginia**. One night, listening through a knothole in a hotel-room door, she overheard the plans of a Northern general. Boyd raced across a battlefield to tell the South's **General Stonewall Jackson**, who turned that information into a big victory in **Front Royal, Virginia**.

SOUTHERN SPIES

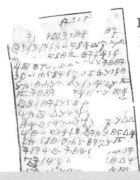

Rose Knows: **Rose Greenhow**, a Southern widow living in **Washington, D.C.**, used her friendships with Northern senators and Secretary of State **William Seward** to discover the North's plans. ← She then sent coded messages southward using the **Secret Line**, a network of men and women that smuggled reports out of the Capitol.

After President Abraham Lincoln was shot and killed in 1865, a $5 Confederate bill was found in his wallet.

iPuzzle
North Decoder

Harriet Tubman received no pay for her work as
a Northern spy and sold homemade items to make
ends meet. Use the key to reveal what those items were.

South Decoder

Use the same key to reveal Belle Boyd's nickname.

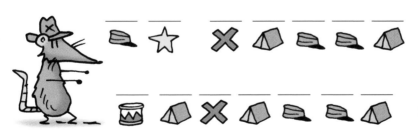

Jump to this
page **or** follow
the pipes.

1925

Where: Nome, Alaska, which has been hit by a deadly disease. The town's only hope—dogs!

Mushin' Impossible

On January 21, Nome's only doctor, **Curtis Welch**, faced a big problem. Two children had just died of **diphtheria** and more cases loomed. His only supply of **serum** (medicine) had expired, and all of Nome's kids were at risk.

Welch sent out an urgent call for new serum. A hospital in **Anchorage**, 975 miles away, had a supply. But sending it by ship wasn't possible (Nome was iced in) and flying it in was too risky. What was left? Sending it by train to **Nenana**, then ferrying it overland by **dogsled**.

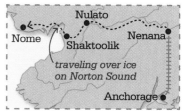

traveling over ice on Norton Sound

Oh, just one problem: Alaska was having its worst winter in 20 years, with howling winds, blizzards, and temperatures dipping to -60° F (-50° C).

On January 27, the first musher (sled driver), **"Wild Bill" Shannon**, and his lead dog, **Blackie**, set off from Nenana with the serum. Sixteen mail-delivery mushers waited along the route in log-cabin **roadhouses** spaced about 30 miles apart (48 km). They would relay the serum, one to the other.

At the same time, champion musher **Leonhard Seppala** and his lead dog, **Togo**, left Nome to intercept the package in **Nulato**. Three days later, as he sped through **Shaktoolik**, a musher coming the other way yelled out, "The serum! The serum! I have it here!" They almost missed each other.

Seppala and his dogs had just traveled 170 miles (274 km), but they turned right around and headed back into a raging storm toward Nome.

Gunnar Kaasen and his lead dog, **Balto**, ran the last leg. Despite hurricane-force winds, blinding snow, and dangerous mountain passes, they pulled into Nome with the serum on February 2. Dr. Welch started giving shots immediately, and instead of a catastrophe, fewer than 10 children in the city died.

Balto photo by Jim Henderson

A statue of Balto in New York City's Central Park

iPuzzle
Togo to Go

We've given you the letters T, O, G, and O. Fill in the blanks to
spell a word or phrase, then match it up with a clue on the right.
Or use the clues to help you figure out the answers on the left.

A. F O R G O T

B. __ O T __ O G

C. __ T O O G __

D. __ O O T __ __ G

E. O __ T __ G O __

F. __ __ __ G __ __ O O T

G. O __ T G __ O __

1. __ Cheering, for a team

2. __ Get too big for

3. A Didn't remember

4. __ Hairy monster

5. __ Frankfurter

6. __ Stop sign shape

7. __ Dope

· EXTRA CREDIT ·

H. T O O __ __ __ G

I. G __ O __ __   T O __ __

J. __ O G O   __ T __ __ __

K. __ O O __ __ __ G __ T

L. __ __ __ O T O G __ __ __ __

8. __ Snapshot

9. __ It helps you see
outside at night.

10. __ Place with no residents

11. __ Toy to jump on

12. __ Handyman's soft-sided carrier

48 Below: While the dogsled teams raced across
Alaska, newspapers in the U.S. (Alaska wasn't a state yet)
followed every detail. On February 1, this headline ran atop
one Cleveland newspaper: NOME TAKES HOPE AS DOGS
DRAW NEAR. Several years later, Balto and his team would
retire to Cleveland, living their last years in…the city's zoo!

Jump to this
page **or** follow
the pipes.

1980

Where: Westport, Connecticut, in the basement of a blue-eyed movie star's barn.

Own Grown

Paul Newman, from a Newman's Own label

Young rats like me know **Paul Newman** as the voice of **Doc Hudson** in the animated movie *Cars*. But he spent decades as one of Hollywood's most famous stars. On the side, he also started up **Newman's Own**, a company that makes popcorn, pizza, lemonade, and many other items—and the most amazing thing happened.

The popularity of those products allowed Newman's company to raise over $370 million to help the needy, the environment, and kids with serious illnesses, to name just a few of the causes it supports.

Newman's Own began by accident. In December 1980 Paul Newman and an old friend, writer **A. E. Hotchner**, mixed up a big tub of salad dressing in his barn. "We didn't have anything to stir it with," Hotchner said, "so Newman went to the river outside the barn and got his canoe paddle." They poured their "oar"iginal dressing into empty wine bottles, then went caroling, giving the stuff out as gifts to their neighbors. It was a big hit—the dressing, not their singing.

When the leftover bottles of dressing sold well in local stores, Newman realized he might have something. Two years later, Newman's Own was launched, introducing America to the first all-natural no-preservatives salad dressing (they didn't use a paddle this time). When, to everyone's surprise, it made $300,000 in profits the first year, Newman declared, "Let's give it all away to those who need it!"

Requests for money started pouring in, some of them a bit goofy. One woman wanted $120,000 so she could move out of her mother's house. No dice. But plenty of deserving causes did get money, anywhere from $250,000 for *The New York Times* Neediest Cases Fund to $500 for a kid taking part in a reading marathon for multiple sclerosis (a nerve-damaging disease).

iPuzzle
Real or Fake?

Four of these Newman's Own products actually exist. Four don't.
Select the ones you think are real, then follow the lines to see if you're right.

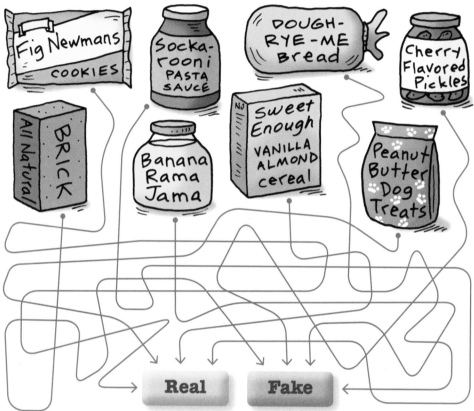

Just Kidding: In 1985 Paul Newman decided he needed to do something more with his Newman's Own profits. He wanted to create a camp for kids with serious illnesses—a place where kids could be kids and have some fun, free of charge. Three years later, the Hole in the Wall Camp opened in Connecticut, later renamed SeriousFun.

Jump to this page **or** follow the pipes.

1869

Where: On Lime Rock island in Newport, Rhode Island's harbor, home to a lone lighthouse.

Rowed Warrior

Quick, name a lighthouse keeper. Don't worry, I couldn't either. But in the late 1800s, lighthouse keeper **Ida Lewis** was famous all across America. Stories of her life-saving feats appeared in national newspapers. She even had a song written about her.

Why all the fuss? Today, March 29, is the day that put Ida Lewis on the map.

It happened at the end of a fierce and frigid afternoon. "I heard the cries of two men during an awful storm," Lewis said. A boat on its way to nearby Fort Adams had capsized, dumping two soldiers into the icy water. Not stopping to put on shoes or a coat, Lewis scrambled into a rowboat. Her little brother joined her. "I could see them clinging to their frail boat," she said.

Lewis pulled hard against the churning waves, testing her claim that she could "row a boat faster than any man in Newport." One of the men in the water, Sergeant Adams, said, "When I saw the boat approaching and a woman rowing, I thought, 'She's only a woman, and she will never reach us.' But I soon changed my mind."

After hauling the two soldiers into the rowboat, Lewis turned back toward land. It took twice as long, the storm now in her face. Once ashore, Sgt. Adams staggered out of the boat, while the other man had to be carried out unconscious. Lewis's feet were blocks of ice.

Although that rescue made Lewis famous, it wasn't her first. In 1858, at age 16, she saved the lives of four boys whose boat had overturned. And it wasn't her last. At age 63, she pulled a friend out of the water, officially her eighteenth life saved.

Home of Ida Lewis

"The Bravest Woman in America"

The Lime Rock Lighthouse was renamed Ida Lewis Lighthouse in 1924.

Ida's full name was Idawalley Zorada Lewis.

iPuzzle
Rowed Work

Find nine differences between the original woodcut
of Ida Lewis, top, and the altered one below it.

Woodcut from *Daughters of America* by Phebe A. Hanaford, 1883

Row, row,
row your
boat,
roughly
through
the waves.

Mightily,
fightily,
doing
rightily,
Ida Lewis
saves!

La, la.

Jump to this
page **or** follow
the pipes.

The Egyptians built a lighthouse in 280 B.C. that was the height of a 40-story building.

1998

Where: South Kivu Province, Democratic Republic of the Congo, soon after the start of the Second Congo War.

"Hello, Africa"

Soldiers have just attacked the village of 5-year-old **Baruani Ndume**. Some of them set Baruani's house on fire, with the boy and his mother inside. Baruani alone survived. "As I was small, I managed to escape through a little hole in the wall," he said later.

An elderly woman from his village helped Baruani make his way to the **Lugufu Refugee Camp** across the border in **Tanzania**.

Living there, Baruani kept his past to himself— for nine long years. Then in 2008, at age 14, he started a radio show with the help of **Radio Kwizera** and **World Vision Tanzania**. It was called *Sisi kwa Sisi* (*Children for Children*). "Boys and girls with stories similar to mine could not easily express themselves and were keeping their pain inside," Baruani said. "Our radio program makes them feel less alone."

The show also gave the children a chance to speak out about problems in the camp. "Sometimes children are denied schooling or food because there are so many people," Baruani said. "I like to ask adults to observe children's rights and to educate children of the camps because it is the way to a better life," he said.

In 2009 Baruani was awarded the **Children's Peace Prize** for his work. The jury said: "Under the most impossible circumstances, Baruani has chosen to champion the rights of other children."

"Hello, Peru"

On December 18, 1944, Maruja Venegas began hosting a children's radio show in Lima, Peru, called *Radio Club Infantil*. In 2013, at age 98, she was still at it—that's 69 years! And because it's "for children and for the ill," she's never taken a penny for it.

The Democratic Republic of the Congo is the largest country with French as its official language.

iPuzzle
Swahili Swap

Follow the directions to translate each Swahili word into English.

CHAKULA

- Go down to the 1st even number
- Go right to an odd number
- Go down to the 2nd even number
- Go left to an even number
- Go up two spaces:

- _____

CHAKULA	ELIMU	NCHI
1	6	COUNTRY
2	REFUGEE	9
EDUCATION	7	10
3	FOOD	PARENTS
4	ORPHAN	11
5	8	12
WAKIMBIZI	WAZAZI	YATIMA

Swahili is the language Baruani *Ndume* speaks.

ELIMU

- Go down to an odd number
- Go right to an even number
- Go down to an odd number
- Go left to an even number
- Go down to an odd number
- Go right to an even number
- Go up to an odd number
- Go left one space:

- _____

NCHI

- Go down to the 1st odd number
- Go left to an even number
- Go up to an odd number
- Go right to an even number
- Go down to an even number
- Go right to an even number
- Go up five spaces:

- _____

WAKIMBIZI

- Go up to the 1st even number
- Go right to an odd number
- Go up to an odd number
- Go left to an even number
- Go down to the 2nd odd number
- Go right one space
- Go up four spaces:

- _____

WAZAZI

- Go up to an odd number
- Go right to an even number
- Go down to an even number
- Go left to an odd number
- Go up to the 2nd even number
- Go right to an odd number
- Go down two spaces:

- _____

YATIMA

- Go up to the 2nd even number
- Go left to an odd number
- Go down two spaces:

- _____

Jump to this page **or** follow the pipes.

1947

Where: Muroc Army Airfield in California's Mojave Desert with a *human* crash-test dummy.

Colonel Stapp and Oscar Eightball

Dummy Luck

Colonel John Stapp, an Air Force doctor and researcher, has just strapped himself into a rocket-powered sled called the **Gee Whiz**. He wants to find out how fast a person can go—then instantly stop—and come out alive.

Wait, what! Why? Back then, people thought airplane pilots could survive only 18 G's (G's explained on the next page). But Stapp suspected the human body could endure much more. If so, aircraft builders needed to be making much stronger seat belts, ejection seats, and airplanes.

Before Stapp hopped into the Gee Whiz, a 185-pound dummy named **Oscar Eightball** "piloted" 32 test runs. That turned out to be a smart move. During one run, the seat belt failed and Oscar went flying through an inch-thick wooden windshield. His rubber face lay behind on the desert floor.

On Stapp's first run, he experienced only 10 G's. But early the next year, he hit an amazing 35 G's! The tests took a toll—he suffered concussions, cracked ribs, lost dental fillings, and blood-filled eyes—but he'd done it.

Stapp's final and craziest ride came in 1954. He boarded another sled, the **Sonic Wind**, in **New Mexico**. Powered by nine rockets that spewed out a trail of fire, it shot down the track at 632 mph (1,017 kph), creating 46.2 G's! Dubbed "The Fastest Man Alive," Stapp had survived again…although he couldn't see for several days because of all the blood in his eyes. :-(

The information collected from Stapp's efforts resulted in new equipment that ended up saving the lives of countless pilots.

A water trough stopped the Sonic Wind in 1.4 seconds.

WHOOSH

SONIC WIND

Colonel Stapp also promoted automobile safety and the use of seat belts in cars.

iPuzzle
On the Fast Track

We've built a rocket sled and strapped a dummy onto it. We call it the P Whiz. Find a route that this rolling sled can take (rounded-corner turns only) to get from START to END.

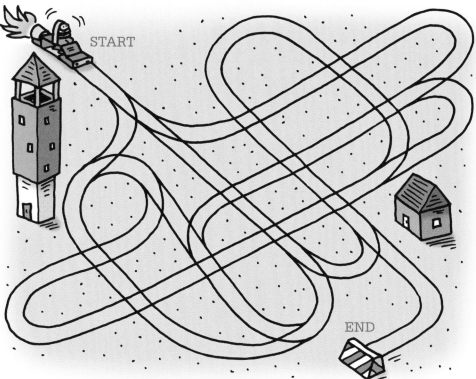

START

END

What is a G? A G is the force of gravity. At sea level you feel one G, which is what makes you weigh what you do. But if you go on one of those loop-the-loop roller coasters, you can feel as much as 5 or 6 G's—you're pushed into your seat as if gravity were five or six times stronger.

Jump to this page **or** follow the pipes.

1992

Where: A whirlwind tour of Brazil, Los Angeles, West Virginia, and Mexico.

Eco-Heroes

Here are my Fave Four planet-protecting people.

Silencer: In 1992 at age 12, Canadian **Severn Cullis-Suzuki** gave a speech at the **Earth Summit** in **Brazil**. As founder of **ECO** (Environmental Children's Org.), she had come to tell adults, "You must change your ways." Severn admitted she didn't have all the solutions. "But neither do you," she said. "If you don't know how to fix it, please stop breaking it." People called her "the girl who silenced the world for five minutes."

Water Girl: In 2004 **Kelydra Welcker**, 15, heard that a chemical from a nearby factory was polluting the water in her hometown of **Parkersburg, West Virginia**. She created a test for detecting the chemical by shaking a water sample in a bottle and measuring the foam. Then she invented a method for cleaning the water using electricity and charcoal. She raised money to **patent** her idea by collecting and recycling 50,000 cans.

Masked Man: El Hijo del Santo is a wrestling superstar in **Mexico**. Wearing a silver mask, he fights bad guys. But in 2007, he joined **WiLDCOAST** to help fight pollution in the **Tijuana River** and to protect **sea turtle** nesting sites, among other causes. He tells his young audiences, "This is the most important fight of my life, and I need all the children to be on my team!"

Gangsta Gardener: Ron Finley of **South Central Los Angeles** calls his neighborhood a "food desert," a place with no access to homegrown food. So, in 2010, he created **L. A. Green Grounds**, which converts vacant lots and strips of scrubby ground into veggie gardens. Residents, homeless people, and kids pitch in to grow plants such as tomatoes and kale. As Finley points out, "If a kid grows kale, a kid eats kale."

It takes 90 percent less energy to recycle an aluminum can than to make a new one.

iPuzzle

Recovery

Number the pictures in order from dirtiest (1) to cleanest (8).

• • • • • • • • EXTRA CREDIT • • • • • • • •

The same string of three letters can complete each of these words:

B _____ M E

D _____ D E

R _____ R D

S _____ N D

Jump to this page **or** follow the pipes.

2008

Where: Mozambique, Africa, where a team of rats has come to nose around.

Squeaky Cleanup

Hup, hup, hup! I'm here to try out for the **HeroRATs**, a team of rodents specially trained to sniff out landmines. I'm not as big as the other candidates—they're all **African giant pouched rats**. But I'm good at smelling things and eating snacks, which is mostly what they do.

The HeroRAT project started 10 years ago, in 1998. A Belgian man named **Bart Weetjens** started it, naming his organization **APOPO**. He decided on rats because they have great noses, they don't weigh enough to set off mines, and they're common in Africa. But enough of that—let's get to work!

Rise and shine! The day starts early. Our human sidekicks lift us out of our clay sleeping jars, and we head out to the field in the HeroRATmobile.

We put on our HeroRAT suits, which are attached to a wire above. Our task is to sniff the ground to locate buried **TNT**, an explosive found in landmines. The other rats are doing great! They scratch the ground when they find a sample and get a banana reward. But I'm finding nothing and going hungry. Fooey!

The graduates will head out to a real minefield in Mozambique's **Gaza Province**. After 16 years of civil war, landmines fill the countryside there, planted by both sides. A lot of people and animals are still getting hurt or killed by them.

In 2011 the HeroRATs finished their job in Mozambique—a year ahead of schedule. They found 2,406 landmines as well as 13,025 weapons and bits of ammunition. And not one person or rat was hurt. As a result, the people of Gaza Province got back a big piece of land that could once again be used for farming, grazing…and living.

iPuzzle
Smells Bad

Seven animals below have a great sense of smell. By comparison, three of them don't smell so well. Each hint will eliminate one or two good smellers (check them off as you go), leaving the three bad smellers.

Eliminate any animal whose name...

...has fewer than 4 letters
...has more than 2 syllables
...has fewer than 2 vowels
...ends in E
...has fewer than 2 syllables

__ Chicken

__ Mole

__ Bear

__ Ant

__ Human

__ Shark

__ Pig

__ Dolphin

__ Snake

__ Elephant

Dr. Rat: In 2008 HeroRATS proved themselves valuable in detecting the deadly disease tuberculosis. They could smell the disease in samples taken from people's throats. Best of all, they can test more samples in 10 minutes than a lab tech can in a day—and do it more accurately.

Year: 2010
Page: **76**
Go Return

Jump to this page **or** follow the pipes.

1992

Where: Mason's Bend, Alabama, home to about 100 people and a few buildings.

Samuel Mockbee ↓

Sweet Home Alabama

Some architects dream of designing fancy homes and important buildings in big cities. Not **Samuel Mockbee**. He and his architecture students build inexpensive houses for poor people in towns that aren't even on some maps. His philosophy: "It's not about your greatness as an architect, but your compassion."

And get a load of some of the materials they use—hay bales, rubber tires, road signs, old bricks, scrap metal, car windshields, and license plates!

Mockbee and Auburn University's **D.K. Ruth** have just started the program, called **Rural Studio**. Twelve **Auburn** architecture students have taken their drawing boards and moved into an abandoned nursing home with Mockbee. Their first project: fix up and enlarge shacks and trailers for the people of **Mason's Bend**.

Since 1992 Rural Studio has completed more than 150 projects. In addition to using unusual materials, the structures also have a sense of style. Mockbee's instructions: "It's got to be warm, dry—and noble."

On one house, **hay bales** filled the walls, a super insulator that cost little. A steeply sloping plastic roof with exposed wooden beams gave the home pizzazz. The next year, the crew used old car tires coated with **stucco** for the walls of an open-air chapel. Its soaring roof was covered in rusted tin shingles.

Mockbee's program wasn't just about building houses. He also believed in building relationships between his students and their older, poorer customers. "It's good to see our students respect clients they wouldn't have acknowledged on the street before," he said. And it went both ways. The homeowners sometimes cooked meals for the students and built warming fires on cold days. They also felt pride in contributing to the students' education.

Alabama means "tribal town" in the Creek Indian language.

iPuzzle

Plate Mate

Old license plates were used for the outer siding on some of the Rural Studio's student dorms. Find two plates below that match.

ALABAMA **78A76** 1990	ALABAMA **8AB06** 1980	ALABAMA **55324** 1965
ALABAMA **78476** 1990	ALAMEDA **55234** 1965	ALABAMA **8AB60** 1980
ALABAMA **8BA06** 1980	ALABAMA **78A67** 1990	ALABAMA **55234** 1965
ALABAMA **55234** 1956	ALABAMA **8AB06** 1970	ALABAMA **78A76** 1909
ALASKA **78A76** 1990	ALI BABA **8AB06** 1980	
ALABAMA **8AB09** 1980	ALABAMA **55234** 1965	

I'm getting dizzy looking!

Year: 1996
Page: 64

Jump to this page **or** follow the pipes.

1864

Where: A train-station platform in Jersey City, New Jersey, as two famous men cross paths.

Hero and Zero

HERO:
Edwin Booth →

At first, **Edwin Booth** didn't measure too high on our **iFlush Hero Meter**. But when I compared the life-saving feat he performed on this wintry Sunday night against what his brother did soon after, I decided he was worth a visit.

Yay!

A crowd of passengers has collected on the train platform to purchase sleeping-car tickets for the overnight trip to **Washington, D.C.** Among them: **Robert Lincoln** (President Abraham Lincoln's eldest son) and Edwin Booth, one of the world's most famous actors at the time.

In the hubbub, Robert Lincoln found himself pushed up against the train, and when it lurched forward, he fell into the gap between it and the platform. Seeing what had happened, Booth dropped his suitcase, grabbed Lincoln by the collar, and pulled him to safety. "That was a narrow escape, Mr. Booth," Lincoln exclaimed, recognizing the actor. Although Booth was a big supporter of Abraham Lincoln, he had no idea he'd just rescued the president's son (he found out later).

Boo!

Hiss!

ZERO:
John
Wilkes
Booth

Less than a year later, Edwin's youngest brother, **John Wilkes Booth**, shot and killed President Lincoln. Edwin was so upset that he didn't act for nearly a year. Not only had the nation lost "a most justly honored and patriotic ruler" but his own brother was the culprit.

Robert Lincoln was the only one of the four Lincoln children to make it to adulthood. The others died of various illnesses. If not for Edwin's action that night in Jersey City, Abraham Lincoln might not have had a single surviving descendant.

CABIN HALL MANOR is an anagram of ABRAHAM LINCOLN.

iPuzzle

iPuzzle
Photo Booth

Here's Edwin Booth looking dashing as Iago in the Shakespearean play *Othello*. Can you find 10 differences between his two poses?

Booth's Return: When Edwin Booth returned to the stage, the public didn't hold the actions of his brother against him. Reporting on his first appearance, the *New York World* wrote, "The men stamped, clapped their hands, and hurrahed continuously; the ladies rose in their seats and waved a thousand handkerchiefs."

Year: 1866
Page: 34
Go Return

Jump to this page **or** follow the pipes.

Bathroom Break

Whew! Time for a rest. While I'm catching my breath, why don't you take a look at four inventions the **Four P's** created specially for this book's heroic adventures.

1.
The Hero Meter

Portia Potty thought this handheld device would help me figure out which heroes I should visit. It did. **Edwin Booth** (on page 46) might not have made the cut without it.

2.
The iFlush Sno-Ball Suit

Plumb Bob designed this for my visit to the **Alps** (see page 60). It inflates like an airbag and is covered with a thick layer of wool. A pair of foam-rubber booties and mittens complete the outfit.

3.
The T.P. Flyer

Air and water power this one-of-a-kind flying vehicle. **Phyllis Tanks** made it using nothing but T.P. and spare bathroom parts. Alas, she couldn't downsize it to fit through sewer pipes, but I did use it to fly to a nearby library for some of my research.

Tail provides stability.

Soap-dish pilot's seat

Up-down and side-to-side control levers

Plunger head acts as a scoop feeding air through a hollowed-out handle.

Superheated water is blasted out of two jets, shooting the T.P. Flyer forward.

A trail of toilet paper makes the T.P. Flyer look snazzy streaking across the sky.

An extractor removes water from the air, then heats it to a nearly steamlike state.

4.
The Turbo-Chair

Not much explanation needed here. **P. Liddy** took a standard **wheelchair** and added a turbo-charged engine and flashy exhaust pipes. It can be seen in use on page 50.

FWIZZZ

Year: 1952
Page: 54
Go   Return

Jump to this page **or** follow the pipes.

2004

Where: Cape Town, South Africa, home of a determined 9-year-old girl.

Big Wheel

The **Four P's** built me a turbo-charged wheelchair for this visit. Why? So I could keep up with **Chaeli Mycroft**.

From left to right: Tarryn, Erin (standing), Chaeli, Justine, and Chelsea

Chaeli (pronounced Kaylee) was born with **cerebral palsy**, which limits the use of her arms and legs. She wanted a motorized wheelchair so she could be more independent. But kid-size ones weren't available here, and importing one would cost $3,000. What to do? Chaeli, her sister, and three friends started selling hand-drawn cards and flowerpot kits to raise the money.

It went so well the girls met their goal in only seven weeks! Then, when the donations kept coming, they decided to help other disabled children. The result: The **Chaeli Campaign** now helps more than 3,000 kids each year by buying wheelchairs, hearing aids, and other equipment. It also sponsors physical-therapy programs to improve mobility, speech, and job skills.

A big issue for disabled children in **South Africa** is not being able to take part in everyday activities, including going to school. "My main drive is for differently abled people to be included and accepted," Chaeli said. "We cannot change our disability, but we can change the way people see our disability." The Chaeli Campaign works directly with schools, trying to make that happen.

In 2011, at age 17, Chaeli received the **International Children's Peace Prize** for her efforts. "Winning the prize has given me a platform to do my activism in a way that's going to reach a lot more people," Chaeli said. "A lot of disabled people can't physically voice what they need and what they deserve, and I can."

I have just one question for the Four P's—how do you stop this thinnnnnggggg!

iPuzzle
Miss Quoted

Below are four statements made by Chaeli Mycroft. However,
every other word has been removed, then listed in order on another line.
Figure out which two lines fit together, then write out each statement.

Example: THIS A BRIEF + IS VERY EXAMPLE. = THIS IS A VERY BRIEF EXAMPLE.

1. ARE DIFFERENT WE HAVE NEED BE REGARDLESS HAVING DISABILITY NOT.

2. WE IN OWN AS NOTHING STOP FROM OUR

3. WITH ARE THE WHO OUTSIDE BOX, WE TO.

4. WE ALL AND ALL THE TO ACCEPTED OF A OR

5. LIFETIME IS HAVE BECOME THAT COMPLETELY AND

6. PEOPLE DISABILITIES OFTEN ONES THINK THE BECAUSE HAVE

7. MY GOAL TO DISABILITY SOMETHING IS ACCEPTED EMBRACED.

8. WHEN BELIEVE OUR POWER CHANGE-MAKERS, CAN US ACHIEVING DREAMS.

> "Change-makers" in no. 8 is one word.

⬜ + ⬜ = _____

_____

⬜ + ⬜ = _____

_____

⬜ + ⬜ = _____

_____

⬜ + ⬜ = _____

Jump to this
page **or** follow
the pipes.

_____

1982

Where: Three comic-book characters in the United States and a wedge-headed advertising superhero in Japan.

Super Cheesy

Is there anything tastier than a slice of **cheddar** or a slathering of melted **Swiss cheese**? To a rat like me, no! And I'm not alone. A pawful of cheese-loving **superheroes** think so, too.

Groo the Wanderer (1982): In over 200 comic books, **Groo**, a swordsman with a nose bigger than his brain, roamed from town to town with his faithful dog **Rufferto**. Hardly an issue of the comic went by without Groo mentioning his favorite food—**cheese dip**! The gooey stuff came up so often that fans would send Groo's creator, **Sergio Aragonés**, packages of cheese dip. Lucky guy!

Little Cheese (1983): Trapped in his father's lab one evening, **Chester Cheese** eats a piece of **Lunar Longhorn**, a type of cheese found on the moon. When it gives him the power to shrink, he goes into training. Using the name **Little Cheese**, he soon joins forces with **Captain Carrot and his Amazing Zoo Crew** to fight crime.

Combo™ Man (1996): While trying to steal a copy of a midterm exam, teenager **Rick Wilder** gets zapped by some bad guys. His backpack is filled with **Marvel comic books** and a bag of **Combos** cheese snacks. Because of that, he takes on the powers of all the superheroes in the comics, becoming Combo Man. It wears off, but he discovers he can transform back into Combo Man by eating another Combos snack. The character was all part of a cheesy ad campaign.

Cheese Zone (2009): Speaking of ads…in a Japanese TV commercial for a cup of curry-flavored noodles, a cheese-headed superhero magically appears and then shoots pieces of cheese from his fingertips into the cup.

Cheese is mentioned three times in the King James version of the Bible.

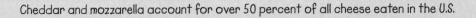
Cheddar and mozzarella account for over 50 percent of all cheese eaten in the U.S.

iPuzzle
Where's My Cheese?

Each cheese in the box is spelled out in one of the sentences below,
with the letters being split between two or even three words.
Circle them as you find them. We did the first to get you started.

CHEDDAR	EDAM	HERVE	ROMANO	~~STRING~~
DERBY	FETA	RICOTTA	STILTON	VENACO

1. WHEN THE CHEESE IS READY, JUST RING FOR ME.

2. EVEN A COUPLE OF CHEESES IS BETTER THAN NONE.

3. CHEESE HAS AN AROMA NO ONE CAN RESIST.

4. THE BIG CHEESE WAS SPOTTED A MILE AWAY.

5. SHE BUNCHED DARK-COATED CHEESES TOGETHER.

6. WE ATE CHEESE AT A CAFE TABLE.

7. MOST CHEESES TILT ONE WAY OR THE OTHER.

8. APRICOT TARTS ARE GREAT WITH CHEESE.

9. HE PUT THE LADDER BY THE CHEESE SHED.

10. I BOUGHT HER VERMONT CHEESE.

iPuzzle Quickie

Match up the jokes
and punch lines.

1. ___ What do you call cheese that isn't yours?

2. ___ What works better than a cheese grater?

3. ___ What cheese is made backward?

A. A cheese gratest.

B. Edam.

C. Nacho cheese.

Jump to this page **or** follow the pipes.

Year: 1992
Page: 16

A farm in Sweden makes cheese from moose milk.

1952

Where: A Seoul, Korea, racetrack, home to Flame, a small female racehorse who's about to join the Korean War.

Horse Power

Reckless with
Sgt. Joseph Latham

Three **Marines** have just purchased **Flame** for $250. A Korean stableboy, the mare's owner, agreed to the deal because he needed the money to buy an **artificial leg** for his sister.

The horse, renamed **Reckless**, quickly fit into Marine life. She ate whatever horse-friendly food could be found— oatmeal, rice straw, and carrots—but she also gobbled up the regular Marine chow. Scrambled eggs were a favorite, in addition to peanut butter sandwiches, mashed potatoes, and chocolate bars. She washed it all down with coffee, cola, or sometimes a beer.

The Marines let Reckless come and go as she pleased. She wandered into tents to watch poker games or to sleep next to the stove on cold nights. The men moved aside to make room.

Her main job was carting ammo to the **recoilless rifles** (shoulder-held weapons) the Marines used in the field. Ignoring explosions all around her, Reckless trudged over long, twisting trails to deliver up to eight of the 24-pound (10 kg) shells at a time. And get this—she did it alone. A Marine would show her the way, then leave her to do her work, all day long. She often carried wounded soldiers back on her return trips.

Her most impressive day came on March 26, 1953, during a battle to retake a hill the Marines called **Vegas**. Reckless made 51 trips, totaling more than 35 miles, carrying nearly five tons of recoilless shells. **Shrapnel** (metal pieces from exploding enemy shells) tore into the flesh above her left eye and flank, but she continued on.

In 1953, **General Randolph Pate** officially made her **Sergeant Reckless**. She lived the last 14 years of her life at **Camp Pendleton** in California.

iPuzzle
Horse Play

END

Find the one trail that will lead Reckless to the hilltop.

POW

Kaboom

Blam

Bam

Bang

BAM

Rice paddy

POW

BANG

START

- -

A Piece of Cake: After arriving in the U.S. on November 10, 1954, Reckless was the guest of honor at a celebration of the Marine Corps's 179th anniversary. She rode an elevator up to the 10th floor of the Marines' Memorial Club in California, then took her place at the head table. Cake was served, but that wasn't enough for Reckless. After finishing her piece, she gobbled up the flower centerpiece.

Year: 1967
Page: 18
Go   Return

Jump to this page **or** follow the pipes.

62

Where: Alexandria, Egypt, home to a clever Greek man known as Hero of Alexandria.

Hero of Alexandria

Was Hero a Hero?

That's a good question. Here's how I figure it. Of all the ancient Greeks who went by the name of Hero—there were around 18 of them!—**Hero of Alexandria** was the most important and famous. So, if someone ranks as the greatest *Hero* of all, he deserves to be part of a hero hunt, right? (Say yes.)

Hero was a math and science genius, but I'm most excited about his cool inventions. Here are three of my favorites:

Aeolipile

Holy water vendor

The **aeolipile** ("wind ball") was the world's first steam-powered engine. When heated, steam shot out of nozzles on a water-filled ball, making it spin. At the time it had no use other than being a fun toy, but locomotives and rockets use the same principle.

Visitors to **Egyptian temples** liked to rinse themselves in **holy water**. They could do that using Hero's **vending machine**. The weight of a coin pushed a lever down, opening a tube that dispensed a dose of the water.

Theater machine

This device put on a play that lasted 10–20 minutes. Sand, weights, ropes, axles, and wheels powered the show from below. At one point, metal balls would drop on a small drum to create the sound of thunder.

Nearly 100 machines and toys are described in Hero's book, Pneumatica.

iPuzzle
H-E-R-O

The letters H, E, R, and O have been filled in. Use the
clues to complete the words, listed in alphabetical order.

Playing pieces are
jumped and crowned on it
1. __ H E __ __ __ R __ O __ __ __

An American Indian tribe
2. __ H E R O __ __ __

The first class students
report to each day
3. H __ __ E R __ O __

Imaginary author of
nursery rhymes (2 words)
4. __ __ __ H E R   __ __ O __ __

African animal with a
horn or two on its nose
5. __ H __ __ __ __ E R O __

Forest for Robin Hood
6. __ H E R __ __ O __

Temperature taker
7. __ H E R __ O __ __ __ __ __

Weather occurrence
with lightning
8. __ H __ __ __ E R __ __ O __ __

Garden carrier that rolls
9. __ H E __ __ __ __ __ R O __

Behold my
treacHEROus
spHEROid.

EXTRA CREDIT: These words are also in alphabetical
order, but separately from the ones above.

Man or woman
who runs a meeting
10. __ H __ __ __ __ E R __ O __

Really sad
11. H E __ R __ __ __ O __ __ __

U.S. President
Hayes
12. __ __ __ H E R __ O __ __

Year: 1057
Page: 26
Go Return

Jump to this
page **or** follow
the pipes.

Hero's book for architects, *Mechanica*, described many ways to lift heavy objects.

1938

Where: Hopping between theaters to catch the premieres of five films about real-life heroes. Hit the lights!

Screen Savers

Boys Town (1938, Omaha, Nebraska): In 1917 **Father Edward Flanagan** built a village in Nebraska dedicated to the care, treatment, and education of homeless boys. When Spencer Tracy won the best-actor **Oscar** for playing Father Flanagan, he dedicated his win to the real Father Flanagan, then sent him the statue.

Serpico (1973, New York City): New York undercover cop **Frank Serpico** discovered widespread corruption on the police force, such as officers taking payoffs from crooks. He told all at a hearing and eventually won the police department's **Medal of Honor**, its highest award. When Serpico wanted to hang out on the set of the movie, the director said no. He thought it would be too distracting.

All the President's Men (1976, New York City): During the 1972 U.S. presidential race, five of **President Nixon**'s men broke into the opposing party's headquarters to get info. *Washington Post* reporters **Carl Bernstein** and **Bob Woodward** exposed the crime and Nixon's involvement in trying to cover it up. The scandal led to Nixon's resignation. Today, the film is often shown to journalism students to inspire them.

Gandhi (1982, New Delhi, India): **Mahatma Gandhi** led India to independence from British rule using nonviolence, noncooperation, and peaceful resistance. **Ben Kingsley,** the star of the movie, looked so much like Gandhi that people walking by the set thought he was Gandhi's ghost.

Erin Brockovich (2000, Los Angeles): Despite a limited education, Erin Brockovich helped win a big legal case against **Pacific Gas and Electric**, proving its chemicals contaminated the drinking water in Hinkley, **California**. In the movie, **Julia Roberts** played Brockovich, while the real Brockovich appeared briefly as a waitress named Julia.

iPuzzle

Real or Reel?

What do these movie heroes do? Make your guesses, then follow the lines to see if you're correct. Continue on to find out whether the film is based on a real person.

Action!

1. ___
Atticus Finch in *To Kill a Mockingbird*

2. ___
Spartacus in *Spartacus*

3. ___
Karen Silkwood in *Silkwood*

4. ___
Indiana Jones in *Raiders of the Lost Ark*

5. ___
Alvin York in *Sergeant York*

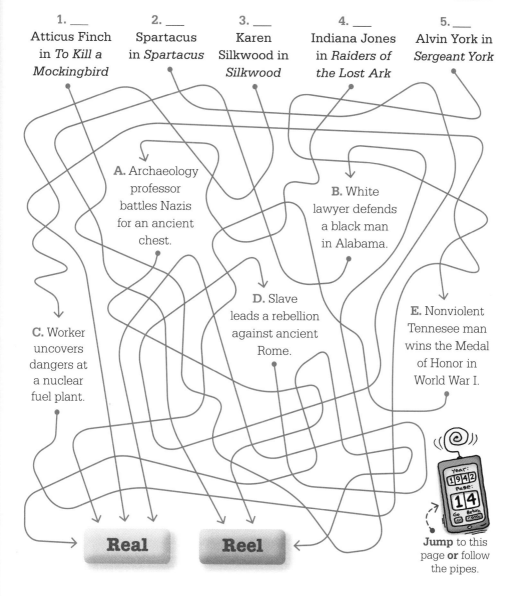

A. Archaeology professor battles Nazis for an ancient chest.

B. White lawyer defends a black man in Alabama.

C. Worker uncovers dangers at a nuclear fuel plant.

D. Slave leads a rebellion against ancient Rome.

E. Nonviolent Tennesee man wins the Medal of Honor in World War I.

Real

Reel

Jump to this page **or** follow the pipes.

Year: 1942
Pase: 14
Go Return

All the President's Men and Erin Brockovich were nominated for Best Picture Oscars, but didn't win.

1805

Where: The Great St. Bernard Pass, a dangerous, snow-covered route through the Swiss Alps.

Snow Fall

Yikes! An **avalanche** just rumbled down the slopes into the pass, and there's snow everywhere. Luckily, I brought my **iFlush Sno-Ball Suit** along. It's keeping me warm as I watch **Barry**, a **St. Bernard dog**, look for survivors.

In the 11th century, a monk named **St. Bernard** established a monastery and lodge here in the pass. Ever since, monks have been helping travelers, or rescuing them when things go wrong. In the 17th century, large dogs joined in on their rescue efforts. Those dogs would soon be named for St. Bernard himself.

Barry is famous around these parts. He's saved so many people the monks have lost count…but they think the number is about 40. Today, he's searching for a young mother and son who were traveling through the pass when the avalanche struck. There's no sign of the mother, but look—Barry has already found the boy, unconscious but still alive!

Barry's run off to alert the monks, but when they arrive, they'll realize they won't be able to reach the boy. He's lying on a steep ledge above a ravine. As usual, it'll be up to Barry to save the day.

I've taken a spot where I can watch, and here comes Barry. He inches his way down the slope. To warm the boy up, he lies next to him, then licks his face to try to wake him. It works. But as the boy comes to, he sees where he is and grabs hold of Barry's slobbery neck. That's Barry's cue. He backs up the slope, towing the boy behind. And—hurray!—he makes it. The monks grab hold of the boy and hustle him back to the monastery.

Everyone will soon be congratulating Barry, and a **monument** will one day be put up in France to commemorate the rescue. But for right now, I'm going to give the big slobber-puss a well-deserved pat on the head.

Originally known as the "Alpine dog" or "Alpine mastiff," the St. Bernard dog earned its permanent name in 1882.

iPuzzle
Mix and Match

Each word or phrase below can be spelled by combining two words from the box, then rearranging the letters. For example, SHUN + DO = HOUNDS.

BRAINS	GOES	MONEY	STAR
CANAL	HAVE	RANTED	TONS
COPY	ISLE	SAWS	UNION
CURED	MAST	SLIPS	WORMS

Where does a snowman keep his money?

In a snowbank.

1. SAINT BERNARD = ＿＿＿＿＿＿ + ＿＿＿＿＿＿

2. SNOWSTORM = ＿＿＿＿＿＿ + ＿＿＿＿＿＿

3. RESCUE DOG = ＿＿＿＿＿＿ + ＿＿＿＿＿＿

4. MONASTERY = ＿＿＿＿＿＿ + ＿＿＿＿＿＿

5. AVALANCHE = ＿＿＿＿＿＿ + ＿＿＿＿＿＿

6. MOUNTAINS = ＿＿＿＿＿＿ + ＿＿＿＿＿＿

7. SWISS ALPS = ＿＿＿＿＿＿ + ＿＿＿＿＿＿

8. ICY SLOPE = ＿＿＿＿＿＿ + ＿＿＿＿＿＿

CARCA: In 2011 a short documentary about the Canadian Avalanche Rescue Cat Association was shown as part of the Banff Mountain Film Festival tour. It chronicled CARCA's efforts to use cats to dig out hikers after avalanches. A website followed up with more information…but it was all just a big joke. There was no such organization.

Year: **1861**
Page: **82**

Jump to this page **or** follow the pipes.

2011 **Where:** Toronto, Canada, to follow the world's oldest marathoner as he makes his way around town.

Fauja Singh's nickname

Turbaned Tornado

Picture someone who runs a **marathon**, a race of 26.2 miles (42 km). Did a 100-year-old man in a bright orange turban with a flowing silver beard come to mind? That describes **Fauja Singh**, a Sikh farmer from India competing today in the **Toronto Waterfront Marathon**. It'll be a record if he finishes, since no one that old has ever completed a marathon.

In 2000 Singh ran his first marathon at age 89. He used it as a remedy for the sadness he felt after the death of his wife and one of his sons. "I was more dead than alive after the personal tragedy in my life," Singh admitted. He also used the race to raise 1,400 pounds ($2,200) for **BLISS**, a charity to help premature babies. "The oldest running for the youngest," he joked.

In 2003 Singh raised thousands more for BLISS and other charities while completing *three* marathons, in **London**, **Toronto**, and **New York**. In Toronto, he set a new world record for a 90+ runner: 5 hours and 40 minutes. But the New York marathon might have been an even greater accomplishment.

That race came just two years after Middle Eastern terrorists attacked New York City's **World Trade Center**. Some people in the U.S. were angry with anyone wearing a turban, including **Indian Sikhs**, who had nothing to do with the attack. Singh's story helped change some minds and made his own people proud. Soon after, he won the **Ellis Island Medal of Honor** as a "symbol of racial tolerance," the first time it was given to a non-American.

Whew, finally! There's the finish line for the 2011 Toronto marathon. The Turbaned Tornado has done it, in 8 hours and 11 minutes. And so have I…barely.

For many years, Fauja Singh was the winner of his village's "catch the chicken" contest.

iPuzzle
Pencil Racing

Get the lead out!

Put your pencil point in an orange circle. Close your eyes and try to draw a line to the red winner's circle. Stop whenever you want, open your eyes, and take a look. If your pencil point isn't in the red circle, close your eyes again, and continue from where you left off.

It counts as 5 seconds each time you open your eyes. Touching or crossing a blue line also adds 5 seconds (if you cross a line, back up to where you crossed it, then take your next turn from there).

100 meters (world record: 15 seconds)

200 meters (world record: 25 seconds)

Obstacle course (iFlush record: 45 seconds)

Invent your own courses on a sheet of paper.

Year: 2012
Page: 70

Jump to this page **or** follow the pipes.

1996

Where: New York City's John F. Kennedy Airport, site of 355,000 annual flights—some made by falcons.

Flight Controllers

John F. Kennedy Airport (JFK) has just hired a **biologist**, Steve Garber, to control the birds that fly around its runways. Every year, flocks of birds smash into airplane windshields and get sucked into engines. Ouch!

JFK isn't alone. Worldwide, more than 250 human lives have been lost from birds hitting airplanes. Billions of dollars in damage have also resulted, not to mention tons of birds biting the dust.

Molly, one of JFK's falcons

Garber's plan: Use **peregrine falcons** to scare flocks away from the airport. "You put a falcon up, and they clear out," head **falconer** John Kellerman said. "It's like putting a shark in the water at the beach."

JFK sits right next to one of largest bird sanctuaries in the northeast, the **Jamaica Bay Wildlife Refuge**. More than 300 bird species hang out there. A small team of **falcons** will work up to 17 hours a day during the warmer months, when bird populations are high. Of particular concern: a **laughing gull** colony in a marsh at the end of two runways.

Animal-protection groups are hoping the falcon plan will work because the previous method, used by the **USDA** (U.S. Dept. of Agriculture), was to shoot the birds. Good news: In 1991, the USDA's shotgun approach cut airplane bird strikes in half. Bad news: 14,191 birds lost their lives. :-(

A big advantage in using falcons is that other birds learn to avoid them. "You don't train a bird to do anything by shooting it," Garber said. Falcons patrolled the skies around JFK for another 14 years. But then, in 2011, the USDA ended the program. Why? It cost too much.

Molly turned gulls into chickens. Hee hee.

iPuzzle

Water Land

In 2009, after taking off from New York's LaGuardia Airport, U.S. Airways Flight 1549 struck a flock of birds and lost both its engines. Captain "Sully" Sullenberger was hailed as a hero for landing the plane on the Hudson River, saving everyone aboard. Find a path of arrows that will land Sully's plane on water.

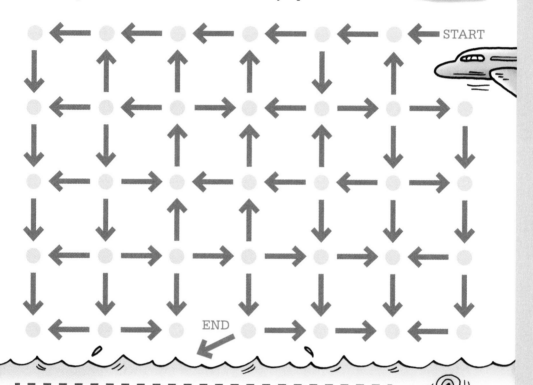

START

END

Fly Away: Airports have come up with lots of ways to try to reduce bird strikes. Here are a few: shooting off fireworks and cannons to scare the birds; replacing grass with gravel; planting bad-tasting grass; filling in ponds; and, at Southwest Florida International Airport, using a Border collie named Jet to chase the chirpers away.

Jump to this page **or** follow the pipes.

1907

Where: Nacozari, a small Mexican mining town that nearly became a huge hole in the ground.

Backtracking

Jesús García Corona

At age 17, **Jesús García Corona** took a job as a water boy for the **Nacozari Railroad**. Its trains traveled from **La Caridad**, a large copper mine outside of town, to Nacozari's **smeltery**, where the copper was separated from rock and other metals.

García moved up quickly, going from switchman to brakeman to machinist. But nobody could have predicted the day that would transform him from rising railroad employee to **Heroe de Nacozari,** "the hero of Nacozari."

It happened on November 7, 1907. The usual railroad engineer, **Alberto Biel**, reported in sick, and 25-year-old García took over the controls. On his first trip to the mine, he noticed hot coals spewing out of the **smokestack**. He reported the problem, which would hopefully be fixed that night. In the meantime, carloads of **dynamite** needed to be delivered to the mine. Uh-oh.

After lunch, García prepared to set out from town for the third time that day. As he did, the wind blew hot coals onto crates of dynamite stacked on the first two cars, setting them on fire. Luckily, dynamite won't explode when burned. But **detonators** packed beneath the crates could, setting off the dynamite! Huge gas tanks and 50 more tons of dyamite stood not far away, endangering the whole town.

García jumped into the engine and jammed the controls into reverse. His plan: to make it to the top of a small hill, where he could jump out and let the train roll off on its own. He came up just short. A huge explosion shook the ground for miles, sending metal, rock, and wood flying in all directions. Jesús García Corona had saved the town and hundreds, if not thousands, of lives…but not himself.

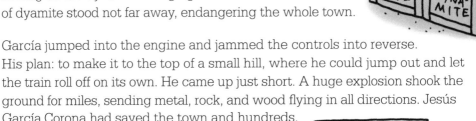

Two years later, the town was renamed **Nacozari de García** in his honor.

iPuzzle
Around and Around

To find out the answer to joke #1, start at the red letter. Write down that letter, C, and then *every other letter*, traveling clockwise. Do the same for joke #2, but starting at the blue letter, T.

1. What do you call a train loaded with packages of gum?

C _ _ _

_ _ _ _

_ _ _ _

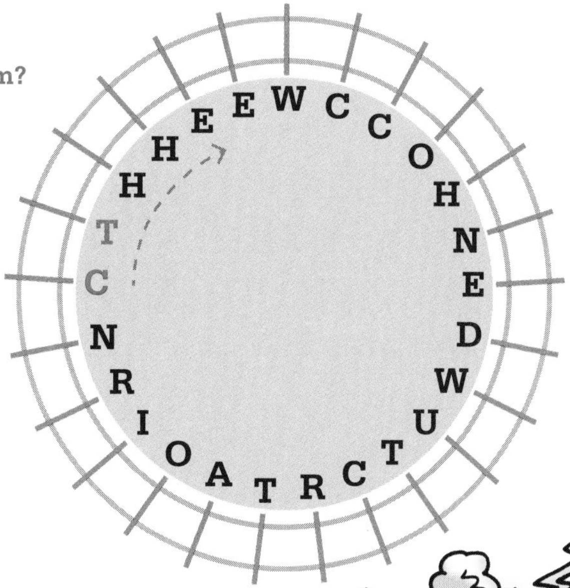

2. Who should you stay away from when a train gets hit by lightning?

_ _ _

WHOO WHOO

COAL

GUM GUM GUM GUM GUM GUM GUM GUM

FRIZZ

Railroader Day: In 1944 the president of Mexico officially made November 7 (the day that Jesús García Corona saved the town of Nacozari) Railroader Day. Honoring both García and railway workers, it's celebrated in many places with speeches, sporting events, and feasts.

Jump to this page **or** follow the pipes.

Year: 1918 Page: 08

1790

Where: Back and forth across the Atlantic to meet a small herd of human-helping critters.

Beast Friends

NC's Finnest (1790, North Carolina): The **Cape Hatteras** inlet is a twisting path that changes with the tides. Before ship captains had navigating gizmos and buoys to help them, there was an albino **dolphin** nicknamed **Hatteras Jack**. Legend has it that when a ship blasted its **foghorn**, Jack would appear and lead the ship through. Once done, he'd celebrate by doing tail walks.

Gorilla My Dreams (1996, Chicago): When a 3-year-old boy fell into the **Brookfield Zoo**'s gorilla exhibit, everyone feared the worst. But a female gorilla named **Binti Jua** picked up the unconscious boy and protectively cradled him in her arms until zookeepers could get in to retrieve him. The boy recovered.

Squeak Up! (1998, England): The Gumbley family's pet rat, **Fido**, awoke one night to discover the house on fire. He managed to unlock his cage, then scampered upstairs to scratch at his owner's door. Once awakened, **Lisa Gumbley**, her two girls, and Fido all made it out alive.

Crime-Fighting Pig (2001, Minnesota): **Becky Moyer** pulled into her garage one night, only to find two stickup men waiting. When she led them inside to get her purse, Moyer's 300-pound **potbellied pig**, Arnold, pounced. He "grabbed the guy's foot and started shaking it until there was blood flying all over," Moyer said. The muggers ran for it, as best they could. Neighbors now call the porker **Arnold the Crime-Fighting Pig**.

Mad Cow (2007, Scotland): When **Fiona Boyd** tried to move a calf and its mother to a shed, the calf cried out. The mother went bull-istic, kicking Boyd to the ground, then rolling on top of her. Boyd's favorite horse, **Kerry**, charged and chased the mooer away, allowing Boyd to roll under the fence to safety.

Two thirds of American households have at least one cat or dog.

iPuzzle
Zoodoku

dolphin fin

rat tail

pig snout

chicken foot

Draw in the missing pictures following the rules in the example.

All 4 pictures in each column

All 4 → pictures in each row

All 4 → pictures in each bold box

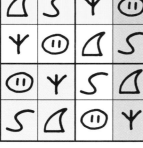

1.

2.

3.

Jump to this page **or** follow the pipes.

2012

Where: Gilda's Club, a building in New York City where kids dealing with cancer are drawing and coloring and laughing.

Spooky Fun

Shhh, don't tell anyone it's me. I've put on my **Mighty Mouse** outfit from page 14, hoping to blend in with all the other superheroes around here. Yikes! **The Hulk** nearly sat on me. Oh, wait, that's just an artist who draws the Hulk, dressed up as him.

What's going on? It's the annual **Halloween** party at **Gilda's Club**, where cartoonists from a group called **The Ink Well** have come to draw with the kids. It's just one of the stops they make each year, mostly at hospitals.

Elizabeth Winter, who has worked on shows like *Rugrats* and *The Wild Thornberrys*, founded The Ink Well in 2005. Her hope was to bring "laughter and creativity to brave kids facing illness." She knows what that's like. "I was diagnosed with cancer as a teenager," Winter said, "and I still remember the long days in the hospital and how having visitors to talk to and make me laugh made all the difference."

It's working. The kids here are having a blast drawing **Batman**, a vampire, **SpongeBob**, and the **Simpsons** with the artists who draw those characters for a living. **Ray Alma**, a comic book and magazine artist, said, "One of my favorite memories at an event was having a child tell me that I draw really well and that I should consider becoming a professional artist."

At another event, **Rami Efal** remembers, "One father took me aside and said it was the first time he'd seen his son smile since he'd come to the hospital." When The Ink Well visited the **Sunrise Day Camp**, for kids with cancer, one boy exclaimed, "This is the best day ever!"

Egad! A cat is reaching for me. Oh, wait, that's just a girl who's had her face painted to look like a cat. She needed a green pencil to draw a witch. Whew!

The Hulk was originally gray, not green.

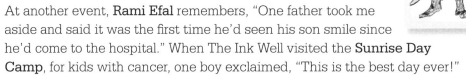

The first Batman comic sold for 10 cents in 1939. In 2010 a collector paid $1 million for one.

iPuzzle
Green Piece

Which two small squares exactly match
squares in Ray Alma's painting of the Hulk?

1.

2.

3.

4.

5.   6.   7.   8.

Jump to this
page **or** follow
the pipes.

2008

Where: Pengzhou, China, a city hit hard by the Sichuan earthquake.

Publicity Hog

MUNCH
MUNCH
MUNCH

Charcoal

Last month, when the **earthquake** struck, flattening towns and killing 69,227 people, things seemed hopeless. That changed just a bit today, thanks to…a **pig**! While clearing the rubble of one house, soldiers discovered a year-old **sow** still alive, pinned there for 36 days. She was soon dubbed **Strong Pig** (*Zhu Jianqiang* in Chinese).

"It's just incredible!" said Pan Banggui, a local **veterinarian**. "No matter how fat a pig is, five days without eating or drinking is its limit." For over a month, Strong Pig drank rainwater and munched on charcoal, nonnutritious but filling. Her weight fell from 330 lbs. (150 kg) to a scrawny 110 lbs. (50 kg).

Strong Pig

MUSEUM MAP

People across China hailed her as a symbol of never giving up. She soon hogged first place in an online poll of "10 animals that moved China in 2008," and millions prayed she'd be spared from the butcher's knife.

It worked. The nearby **Jianchuan Museum** paid 3,008 yuan ($492) to buy Strong Pig from her owner, promising to look after her for the rest of her life. "She's not just a pig; she's a hero," a museum official, Wu Zhiwei, said.

Ten thousand visitors flocked to the museum every day to see China's newest star. It went well for the first few months, said staff member Huang Yi. "Strong Pig would still raise its head when reporters and visitors came to take photos." But things went downhill fast. As the pig bulked up, reaching 440 lbs. (200 kg), she got lazier. "Now, it just blocks the door to its bedroom when there are too many visitors outside," Huang said.

Strong Pig's popularity dropped, but that didn't stop researchers at a nearby lab from **cloning** her. Six piglets resulted, but only time will tell if they inherited Strong Pig's legendary will to survive.

Strong Piglets

There are about 2 billion pigs in the world.

iPuzzle

Uplifting

Use *either* the letters in **PIG** or the letters in **HOG**,
in any order, to complete each word.

1. T __ __ H T R O __ E   2. S __ __ A __ H E T T __

3. N E I __ __ B __ R   4. T __ N I __ __ T

5. __ E N __ U __ N   6. S __ R __ N __

7. __ A V __ N __   8. __ __ T D O __

9. __ R __ W T __   10. T __ U __ __

11. __ R __ __ E   12. __ __ __ S T

Spotlighting two geographic locations:

13. C __ I C A __ __   14. __ __ T T S B U R __ H

EXTRA CREDIT: Use *both* **PIG** and **HOG**
to complete *each* of these words:

15. S __ __ T L I __ __ T __ N __   16. __ E __ __ R A __ __ __ C

iPuzzle Quickie

Match up the jokes
and punch lines.

1. ___ Who is the world's smartest pig?

2. ___ What do pigs use to write secret messages?

3. ___ What do you call pig thieves?

A. Hamburglars.

B. Ein-swine.

C. Disappearing oink.

Jump to this page **or** follow the pipes.

Year: 2008
Page: 42

Pigs like to wallow in mud because they have no sweat glands to keep themselves cool.

1944

Where: Camp Forrest, Tennessee, an army training base with a bunch of soldiers blowing things up…with air.

Highway Rubbery

An inflatable tank being carried into position

Army recruiters have been combing America to staff a special **World War II** unit whose mission won't be to fight, but to fool the enemy. Among the weapons they'll use: inflatable rubber tanks, "spoof" radio messages, and phony sound recordings of army equipment and troops.

Photo by the U.S. Army

Although officially known as the **23rd Headquarters Special Troops**, many people call the unit the **Ghost Army**. It consists of 1,100 artists, architects, set designers, movie people, engineers, and sound wizards who can create the illusion of 30,000 troops and their equipment — there one day, gone the next!

The Ghost Army performed 21 operations following **D-Day**, the Allied invasion of **France** on June 6, 1944. At the western port of **Brest, France**, they set up 50 rubber tanks, drove trucks around in loops, and set up fake artillery. It helped the Allies win control of the port.

On the other side of France, in **Metz**, **General Patton**'s **Third Army** was unprotected to the north. The Ghost Army rushed in, set up its dummy equipment, sent phony radio messages, and broadcast the sounds of troop movements all night long. They fooled the Germans for seven days and kept them from attacking until real troops arrived.

The unit's secret insignia, never worn in action

The Ghost Army's final operation came at the **Rhine River** at **Viersen, Germany**. They pulled out all the stops, creating fake airstrips, buildings,

and bridges. They lit phony campfires at night, put up fake troop-directing traffic signs, and impersonated officers at local bars, hoping spies would overhear them talking. It worked. The Germans massed their troops opposite the Ghost Army. Meanwhile, the **Ninth Army**'s real troops met little resistance to the south, saving an estimated 10,000 American lives.

The famous fashion designer, Bill Blass, was a member of the Ghost Army.

iPuzzle

Tanks a Lot

Find the pair of real tanks below, the only two that match identically.
All the others are rubber inflatables created by the Ghost Army.

1.
2.
3.
4.
5.
6.
7.
8.
9.

Lumbering: At one point during World War II, the RAF
(Great Britain's air force) discovered the Germans building
a decoy airfield, complete with fake wooden airplanes. The
Brits waited until the work was completed, then sent a
single airplane to drop a phony wooden bomb on the site.

Year: 1946
Page: 86
Go / Return

Jump to this
page **or** follow
the pipes.

2010

Where: Abu Dhabi, capital of the United Arab Emirates (UAE) on the Persian Gulf.

S̶t̶opping Bags

Abdul Muqeet, age 8, doesn't like plastic bags. It all began when his principal announced a "No Plastic" day at school. "So I came to my house," Adbul said, "and I asked my mom, 'Why should I not use the plastic bags?'"

The answer: Half a *trillion* **plastic bags** are made every year, each of which will last a thousand years. The oceans are overloaded with plastic litter—bags, bottles, and tons more. In the **Pacific Ocean** alone, there are several giant "garbage patches" clogging the water.

"In one year, one million sea creatures die because of plastic," Abdul points out. "If [it's] harming the environment so much, why are we even using it?"

That's when Adbul had an idea. "Why can't we recycle old newspapers and start making bags?" he said. He set to work. "I was thinking that maybe after ten or fifteen days he will stop," his father said. "But he did not. He tried to make more and more and tried to fine-tune it." Abdul made 4,000 bags the first year, which he distributed to shops for free. He led workshops at schools and companies, inspiring others to stop using plastic bags and to use or make their own "Mukku bags" instead (Mukku is his nickname).

In 2011 the **Crown Prince** of Abu Dhabi gave Abdul the **Abu Dhabi Award**, for exceptional service to the state. And later that year, the United Nations invited the "Paper Bag Boy" to spread the word at its **Tunza conference** in **Indonesia**, a gathering of young people to discuss environmental issues.

- - - - -

Bag Lunch

In 2009 a 16-year-old Canadian student, Daniel Burd, won the Canada-Wide Science Fair by identifying rare microbes that can break down plastic bags by 40 percent in only six weeks.

Abu Dhabi is the largest of seven emirates (principalities) that make up the United Arab Emirates.

Plastic bags first appeared in the 1950s. Most of them still exist.

How quickly can you solve all 3 puzzles?

iPuzzle
Grab Bag

A.

Spell a dozen words using only the letters in **ENVIRONMENT**.
English words only, at least three letters long, and no proper names.

_____   _____   _____   _____

_____   _____   _____   _____

_____   _____   _____   _____

B.

Match up each word or phrase on the left with a wacky anagram
of it on the right (the same letters in a different order).

1. ___ ABDUL MUQEET   **A.** A DENTIST UNION

2. ___ CROWN PRINCE   **B.** ACE PICNIC OAF

3. ___ EMIRATES   **C.** BALTIC GASP

4. ___ NEWSPAPERS   **D.** CORN CREW PIN

5. ___ PACIFIC OCEAN   **E.** EQUAL MUD BET

6. ___ PLASTIC BAG   **F.** LOCAL PRISON CHIP

7. ___ SCHOOL PRINCIPAL   **G.** STEAMIER

8. ___ UNITED NATIONS   **H.** WE SNAPPERS

C.

The phrases below are anagrams of each
other. They're also an anagram of what
two-word phrase on the previous page?

PUNIER FLAGS • SINFUL GRAPE
RUG LIFESPAN • PIG FUNERALS

Jump to this
page **or** follow
the pipes.

1973

Where: Rushville, a small town in Illinois where it'll cost you $2 to see the doctor. If you don't have it, he'll see you anyway.

Dr. Too-Little

It's 10:00 a.m., and patients are packed into **Dr. Russell Dohner**'s waiting room. Many of them are unemployed with no health insurance. That doesn't matter. Two dollars will cover the visit—no appointment, no bill, no forms to fill out. If you're really sick, come around to the back door for immediate attention.

I chose 1973 so I could save a few bucks.

I know what you're thinking: Things were cheap in 1973. But not that cheap. Forty years later, Dr. Dohner charges only $5 (yes, he's still at it). "I never went into medicine to make money," he said. "I wanted to be a doctor, taking care of people."

Dr. Dohner grew up on a farm in **Rushville**, graduated from **medical school** in 1955, and then returned home to help the town's doctor. He figured the job would last a few years; his dream was to become a big-city heart doctor. But then the other doctor quit. "Rushville needed a doctor, so I stayed," Dohner said. And never left.

Over the years, he's delivered 3,500 babies, more than the population of Rushville. He makes house calls, daily rounds at the local hospital, and regular visits to area nursing homes. In 55 years he's never taken a vacation or even a full day off. "What if someone needs me?" he asks.

A Whirlwind Tour

On November 23, 2004, another small-town doctor, Dr. Kenneth Mauterer, was set to receive the "Country Doctor of the Year" award in his hometown of Olla, Louisiana. But a fierce tornado struck, and he ended up spending the entire night tending to the injured at their homes and in the local hospital. The award seemed even more deserved when he finally received it two months later.

iPuzzle

Price Check

Match up the 10 items with their 1973 prices. Then use the PRICE CHECKER at the bottom to see how you did. More than five correct is great. If you get all 10, I have just one question: How old are you?

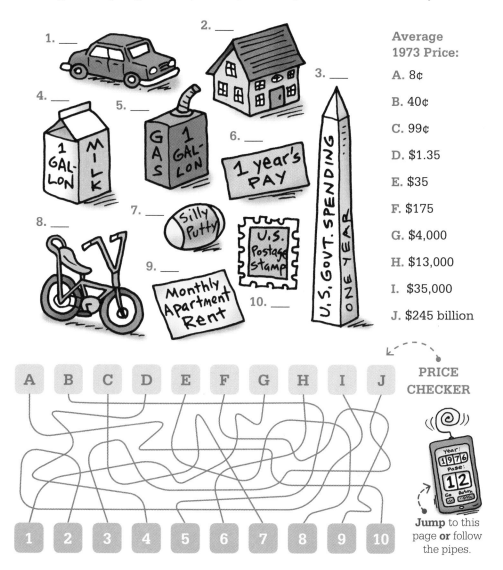

Average 1973 Price:

A. 8¢

B. 40¢

C. 99¢

D. $1.35

E. $35

F. $175

G. $4,000

H. $13,000

I. $35,000

J. $245 billion

PRICE CHECKER

Jump to this page **or** follow the pipes.

1997

Where: At a public school in Brooklyn, New York, home to the national champs…in chess.

Board Gamers

Welcome to **Intermediate School 318**, an inner-city middle school of mostly black and hispanic students. Over 70 percent of the families here live below the national poverty level, yet their kids are some of the best **chess** players in the country.

How did that happen? It began in 1997 with a program called Chess Nuts. Just 10 students participated. But interest grew until nearly half of the school's 1,600 students were taking chess classes. "In some schools," Principal **Fred Rubino** said in a 2009 documentary, *Brooklyn Castle,* "if you're on the chess team…no one wants anything to do with you. At 318, the geeks, they are the athletes."

Elizabeth Spiegel is the guiding force behind that success. She joined the school in 1999 as a once-a-week chess teacher. That became full-time after earning her teaching degree. Assistant Principal **John Galvin** acts as the team's manager.

In 2000, 318's chess team traveled to Arizona for their first **National Junior High Championship**. They won in the beginner's division. They did even better the next year and, in 2004, took home the top prize as the best team in the country. Their competition—mostly rich communities and private schools with big budgets.

By 2012, 318's chess team had won more than two dozen national championships. Then came what Galvin called "the culmination of a decade of hard work." The middle school whizzes of 318 competed in the *high school* national championship…and won! "It had never happened before," Galvin said, "and probably never will again."

Home of the National chess champs

iPuzzle
We're No. 1

What school has won more junior-high national chess championships than any other? Do the math.

What does an Australian chess player say before leaving a restaurant?

A
Circle a number:

1 2 3 4 5 6
7 8 9 10 11 12

Check, mate.

The number circled in A →

B
A × 2 =

C
B + 6 =

D
C ÷ 2 =

The Answer:

Where's the best place to buy a used chess set?

E
D − A =

F
E × 6 =

A pawn shop.

Grandmaster: Six years before I.S. 318 started their chess program, Maurice Ashley, the world's first and only black chess grandmaster, had success in another low-income neighborhood. He coached the Raging Rooks of Adam Clayton Powell Jr. Junior High in Harlem, New York, to the 1991 national championship.

Year: **1998**
Page: **36**
Go   Return

Jump to this page **or** follow the pipes.

1861 **Where:** A hospital for Union troops in Cairo, Illinois, during the Civil War.

Mother Figure

Don't mess with **Mary Ann Bickerdyke**, known around here as "Mother." She has one aim: to help the wounded and sick—and anyone who gets in the way is going to be sorry.

Arriving in **Cairo** in June, Bickerdyke discovered a field of tents filled with dying soldiers in filthy clothes eating lousy food and having no bathrooms to use. That was the hospital! When the head doctor proved unwilling to do anything about it, Mother Bickerdyke told him, "You make me sick!" and took charge. She scrubbed the soldiers, cleaned the tents, and served home-cooked meals.

When the army decided to convert a local hotel into a military hospital, the bossy Bickerdyke ordered the carpenters to work faster. Once they finished, she moved in. The head doctor ordered her to leave. Mother refused. "I'm here as long as the men need me. If you put me out one door, I'll come in another…and the patients will help me in." **General Ulysses S. Grant** knew a good thing when he saw it. He asked that Bickerdyke be made the hospital manager, which the doctor begrudgingly did.

When Bickerdyke discovered the hospital staff was eating food intended for the patients, she set a trap. She placed freshly baked peaches topped with **vomit medicine** on a window sill to cool. "See that nobody touches 'em," Mother told the cook. "This is patients' food." You guessed it—the staff was soon puking up peaches.

Another time, Bickerdyke spotted a young lieutenant wearing a clean shirt sent specifically for use by the patients. A room full of sick and wounded men cheered as Mother wrestled him to the ground, then sat on him and pulled the shirt off.

Bickerdyke traveled with the army to 19 battles over the next four years. Along the way, she helped set up 300 hospitals. But no matter where she went, Mother always had the last word.

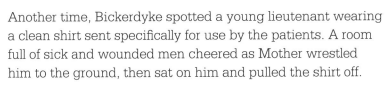

During World War II, a cargo ship was named SS *Mary Bickerdyke*.

iPuzzle
Find Mother

Find the one path of circles that spells **BICKERDYKE**.

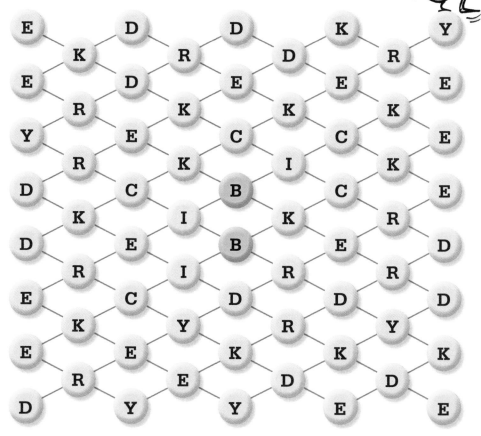

The Boss: In 1863, Mother Bickerdyke offended a colonel's wife because she wouldn't leave wounded troops to help the woman's boy, who had the measles. When the colonel complained to General William T. Sherman, saying a "nasty old woman" named Bickerdyke had yelled at his wife, the general replied, "Oh, well, this is too bad. You've picked on the one person around here who outranks me."

Jump to this page **or** follow the pipes.

1886

Where: On the paper-strewn streets of Broadway in lower Manhattan.

Paper Route

Welcome to a place where heroes are measured by how much ticker-tape trash they create. It all started today, October 28, after **President Grover Cleveland** dedicated the **Statue of Liberty**.

A parade of officials, marching bands, and 20,000 French soldiers started at 23rd Street, in a park where the Statue of Liberty's arm had been displayed for six years, and headed downtown. As the procession passed near the **New York Stock Exchange**, financial workers joined in the celebration by throwing paper **ticker tape** out their windows.

Stock tickers spewed out paper ticker tapes with the latest stock prices on them.

That started a tradition that's been followed ever since. And New York City's **Department of Sanitation** has been keeping track of how much paper it's had to sweep up the next day.

Early ticker-tape parades focused on foreign leaders and military VIPs. About 1,000 tons of paper covered the streets after each of those. In 1927, after **Charles Lindbergh** flew solo across the **Atlantic**, he was showered with 1,750 tons of ticker tape. That was nothing compared to **General Douglas MacArthur**'s 1951 total when he returned home after years of war in **Asia**—3,429 tons.

The oddest honoree? That would have to be **Aimé Tschiffely** in 1928, after he completed a three-year horse ride from **Argentina** to **Washington, D.C.** Apparently, nobody even bothered to weigh his trash total.

And the winner? **John Glenn** attracted 3,474 tons of ticker tape after becoming the first American to orbit Earth. But fame is fleeting. Thirty-six years later, a second parade to honor Glenn as the oldest person in space (age 77) racked up the lowest amount ever—12.9 tons.

Over the years, New York City has hosted over 200 ticker-tape parades.

iPuzzle
Ticker-Tape Trail

Find the one route from START to END.

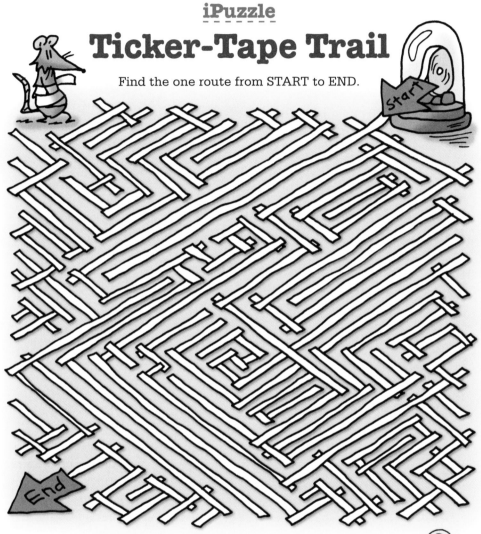

Heap Big Fun: New York City's largest-ever trash-producing event came when World War II ended in 1945. Starting on August 14, a two-day celebration in Times Square left behind a sea of paper, feathers, cloth, and hat trimmings totaling 5,438 tons.

Jump to this page **or** follow the pipes.

The section of Broadway where most ticker-tape parades are held is called the "Canyon of Heroes."

1946

Where: Western Pennsylvania, to check out a car trunk of items for sale.

My "Fair" Lady

No, it's not illegal stuff. **Edna Ruth Byler** has just returned from **Puerto Rico**, and her trunk is filled with pieces of **needlework**—beautiful designs sewn into linen with needle and thread.

After seeing the widespread poverty in Puerto Rico, Byler had an idea. What if she paid some of the local women a fair price for their work and sold the items in the United States?

Here's how Byler set things up. She determined the cost of the women's materials, then added in a fair wage for the time and skill required to make a finished piece. Any profits went directly toward buying more crafts in other low-income countries (next up: woodwork from Haiti). Her plan worked, helping to launch the concept of **fair trade**.

Nearly 70 years later, Byler's car trunk is likely rusting away in some Pennsylvania junkyard, but her idea has grown into a nonprofit organization known as **Ten Thousand Villages**. It operates nearly 400 shops selling handmade jewelry, gifts, and other items from artists in Latin America, Asia, Africa, and the Middle East.

Ten Thousand Villages encourages the use of recycled and natural materials, and sometimes gives suggestions to its suppliers for products that might prove popular. The organization establishes long-term relationships with artists and pays in full when their creations leave the country. The result—talented people who would otherwise be unemployed or underemployed get a fair chance to create a better life for themselves.

Fairly Tricky

Fill in the words to complete these 10 tongue twisters,
then try saying each phrase three times fast.

1. EDNA __ __ __ __ __ EARLY   A. AFTER

2. TEN __ __ __ __ __ __ __ __ HENHOUSES   B. BYLER'S

3. VILLAGE __ __ __ __ __ __ __ __   C. ENDED

4. __ __ __ __ __ __ BARRELS   D. FAIR

5. FEAR __ __ __ __ FINES   E. HAITI

6. RECYCLE __ __ __ __ __ __ __ __ __   F. NEEDLES

7. NEEDLESS __ __ __ __ __ __ __   G. RESOURCES

8. __ __ __ __ __ AFRICA   H. SPILLAGE

9. __ __ __ __ __ TRUNKS   I. THOUSAND

10. EIGHTY HOT __ __ __ __ __ HUTS   J. TRUCK

iPuzzle Quickie

Use the clues to complete these words
and phrases that start with FAIR.

1. Made-up story: F A I R __ __ __ __ __ __

2. Umpire's cry: "F A I R __ __ __ __ __ !"

3. Good TV forecast: F A I R __ __ __ __ __ __ __

4. Part of a golf course: F A I R __ __ __

Jump to this
page **or** follow
the pipes.

The End

Well done! You've made it to page 88, something not many other kids can say. (It's not that other kids haven't made it here—it's just that we won't let many of them say it.)

It's a First!

In our two previous books, *Swimming in Science* and *Hurtling thru History*, we promised there would be no asparagus and no liverwurst. But we goofed. There were stalks and tubes of those supposedly foodlike substances littering each book.

But we didn't make that same mistake this time! On the cover and title page, we promised no anchovies, and—go ahead and look—there's not a single anchovy mention or sighting anywhere within these pages. Oh, wait, I just blew it, didn't I?

Moving Right Along

As usual, the Four P's have concocted a final quiz for you on the next page. What are you waiting for—get cracking!

Any favorite heroes from the book?

Other than me, that is!

Let me know at: dwayne@bathroomreader.com

Bravo!

iPuzzle

Ridiculous Quiz

1. Which of these is not a harmful food additive eaten by the Poison Squad?

   a. ___ formaldehyde

   b. ___ copper sulfate

   c. ___ anchovies

2. What are anchovies?

   a. ___ salted fish found in breakfast cereal

   b. ___ the best pizza topping ever!

   c. ___ the correct answer to question No.1

3. What is Pikachu?

   a. ___ something you say when you sneeze

   b. ___ the dictionary entry right after "peek-a-boo"

   c. ___ a mouselike video-game critter

4. How is Chaeli Mycroft's first name pronounced?

   a. ___ Chaylee

   b. ___ Cha Eli

   c. ___ Kaylee

5. Which dummy "piloted" 32 test runs of the U.S. Air Force's Gee Whiz rocket sled?

   a. ___ Plumb Bob

   b. ___ Phyllis Tanks

   c. ___ Oscar Eightball

6. Which of these is a brother of the famous 19th-century actor Edwin Booth?

   a. ___ Voting Booth

   b. ___ Phone Booth

   c. ___ John Wilkes Booth

Answers

9. Pigeon Towed

3 leads to the headquarters (HQ) tent.

11. Milk Made

A. OINK
B. ILL
C. MARCH
D. LAKE
E. TOM

HOLE MILK (whole milk)
A MILK CARTON

15. Rodent Chase

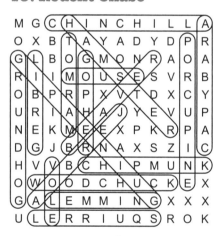

17. Iqbal Masih

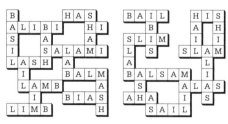

19. Partner-Ship

3 and 8 are exactly the same.

21. Cowabunga

1. C	2. E	3. F	4. G
5. B	6. I	7. H	8. J
9. A	10. D		

23. Trail Mix

1. D	2. E	3. B	4. F
5. C	6. H	7. A	8. J
9. I	10. G		

25. Soup-Doku

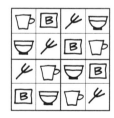

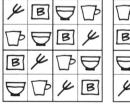

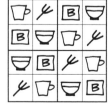

27. Take a Bao

包拯拯包包拯拯拯包包包拯拯
包拯包拯包拯包拯包拯包包包
包包包拯拯包包拯拯包包拯拯
拯包包包拯包拯拯包包拯包拯
包拯拯拯包包包拯拯拯包包包
包包拯拯包拯拯拯包包包拯包
拯包包包拯包包拯拯拯包包拯
包包拯拯包包拯拯包拯拯拯包
包拯拯包拯包包拯拯包拯包拯
包拯拯拯包包拯包包包拯包包

29. North Decoder

PIES, ROOT BEER, GINGERBREAD

South Decoder:

LA BELLE REBELLE

31. Togo to Go

1. D ROOTING
2. G OUTGROW
3. A FORGOT
4. F BIGFOOT
5. B HOTDOG
6. E OCTAGON
7. C STOOGE

Extra Credit:

8. L PHOTOGRAPH
9. K MOONLIGHT
10. I GHOST TOWN
11. J POGO STICK
12. H TOOLBAG

33. Real or Fake?

Real:
Fig Newmans cookies
Sockarooni pasta sauce
Sweet Enough vanilla almond cereal
Peanut butter dog treats

35. Rowed Work

37. Swahili Swap

CHAKULA = FOOD
ELIMU = EDUCATION
NCHI = COUNTRY
WAKIMBIZI = REFUGEE
WAZAZI = PARENTS
YATIMA = ORPHAN

39. On the Fast Track

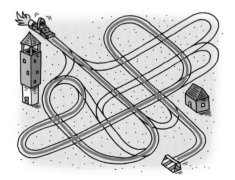

41. Recovery

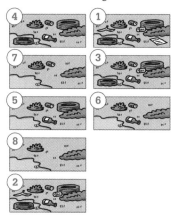

Extra Credit: ECO—become, decode, record, second

43. Smells Bad

The three bad smellers are the chicken, human, and dolphin.

45. Plate Mate

This plate, the third one down in the third column and the last one in the middle column:

> **ALABAMA**
> **55234**
> **1965**

47. Photo Booth

1. buttons on cap
2. feathers in cap
3. small beard
4. ruffled white collar
5. vest opening
6. vest sleeve
7. belt
8. length of cane
9. angle of right leg
10. strap on left shoe

51. Miss Quoted

4 + 1 = We are all different and we all have the need to be accepted regardless of having a disability or not.

7 + 5 = My lifetime goal is to have disability become something that is completely accepted and embraced.

8 + 2 = When we believe in our own power as change-makers, nothing can stop us from achieving our dreams.

6 + 3 = People with disabilities are often the ones who think outside the box, because we have to.

53. Where's My Cheese?

1. …JUST RING_FOR ME.
2. EVEN A COUPLE OF…
3. …AN AROMA NO ONE…
4. …SPOTTED A MILE AWAY.
5. SHE BUNCHED DARK-COATED…
6. …AT A CAFE TABLE.
7. MOST CHEESES TILT ONE…
8. APRICOT TARTS…
9. HE PUT THE LADDER BY THE…
10. I BOUGHT HER VERMONT…

iPuzzle Quickie:

1. C   2. A   3. B

55. Horse Play

57. H-E-R-O

1. CHECKERBOARD
2. CHEROKEE
3. HOMEROOM
4. MOTHER GOOSE
5. RHINOCEROS
6. SHERWOOD
7. THERMOMETER
8. THUNDERSTORM
9. WHEELBARROW

Extra Credit:

10. CHAIRPERSON
11. HEARTBROKEN
12. RUTHERFORD

59. Real or Reel?

1. B—Reel
2. D—Real
3. C—Real
4. A—Reel
5. E—Real

61. Mix and Match

1. BRAINS + RANTED
2. WORMS + TONS
3. GOES + CURED
4. MONEY + STAR
5. CANAL + HAVE
6. UNION + MAST
7. SAWS + SLIPS
8. COPY + ISLE

65. Water Land

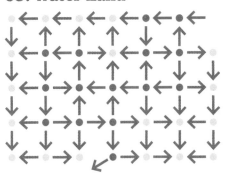

67. Around and Around

CHEW CHEW TRAIN
THE CONDUCTOR

69. Zoodoku

71. Green Piece

3 and 6 are exactly the same as pieces in the full painting.

73. Uplifting

1. TIGHTROPE
2. SPAGHETTI
3. NEIGHBOR
4. TONIGHT
5. PENGUIN
6. SPRING
7. PAVING
8. HOTDOG
9. GROWTH
10. TOUGH
11. GRIPE
12. GHOST

Geographic:

13. CHICAGO
14. PITTSBURGH

Extra Credit:

15. SPOTLIGHTING
16. GEOGRAPHIC

iPuzzle Quickie:

1. B
2. C
3. A

75. Tanks a Lot

4 and 9 are identical. 1. no star
2. angle of gun 3. no panel below gun
5. no hatch at top 6. wind-up key
7. wheel missing in tread 8. antenna

77. Grab Bag

A. Here's our list:

EON	ITEM	TERN	OVERT
EVE	MEET	TIER	REMIT
INN	MERE	TIME	RIVET
ION	METE	TINE	TENON
IRE	MIEN	TIRE	TENOR
MEN	MINE	TOME	TIMER
MET	MINT	TONE	TONER
NET	MIRE	TORE	VENOM
NIT	MITE	TORN	VOMIT
NOR	MORE	TREE	VOTER
NOT	MORN	TRIM	ENTIRE
ONE	MOTE	TRIO	ERMINE
ORE	MOVE	VEER	INTERN
REV	NEON	VEIN	INTONE
RIM	NINE	VENT	INVENT
ROE	NONE	VETO	INVERT
ROT	NORM	VINE	MENTOR
TEE	NOTE	VOTE	METEOR
TEN	OMEN	EMOTE	METIER
TIE	OMIT	ENTER	MOTIVE
TIN	OVEN	EVENT	ORIENT
TOE	OVER	INERT	REMOTE
TOM	REIN	INNER	REMOVE
TON	RENT	MERIT	VERMIN
VET	RIME	METER	EMINENT
VIE	RIOT	MINER	ENVIRON
VIM	RITE	MINOR	MENTION
EMIT	ROTE	MITER	NOMINEE
EVEN	ROVE	MOVER	VINTNER
EVER	TEEM	MOVIE	INVENTOR
INTO	TEEN	NERVE	OVERTIME
IRON	TERM	NEVER	REINVENT

B. 1. E   2. D   3. G   4. H
       5. B   6. C   7. F   8. A

C. Persian Gulf

79. Price Check

1. G   2. I   3. J   4. D   5. B
6. H   7. C   8. E   9. F   10. A

81. We're No. 1

318 (E = 3, F = 18)
No matter what number you circle
in A, E will equal 3 and F will equal 18.

83. Find Mother

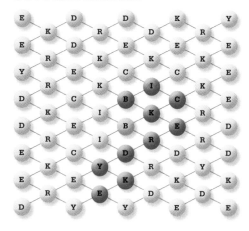

85. Ticker-Tape Trail

87. Fairly Tricky

1. C   2. I   3. H   4. B   5. D
6. G   7. F   8. A   9. J   10. E

iPuzzle Quickie:

1. Fairy tale   2. "Fair ball!"
3. Fair weather   4. Fairway

89. Ridiculous Quiz

The correct answer for each is "c."

iBonus
Make a Super-Rodent

Here's a chance to create your own rodent
superhero. Don't hold back—go nuts!

1. Which Rodent?

A rodent list appears in the
page-15 puzzle. Or, missing
from that list—a rat!

2. Super Outfit?

What does your rodent
wear? Boots? A cape?
A shirt made of bark?

3. Super Powers?

Super-fast gnawing?
Changes by eating acorns?
Travels by tunnel?

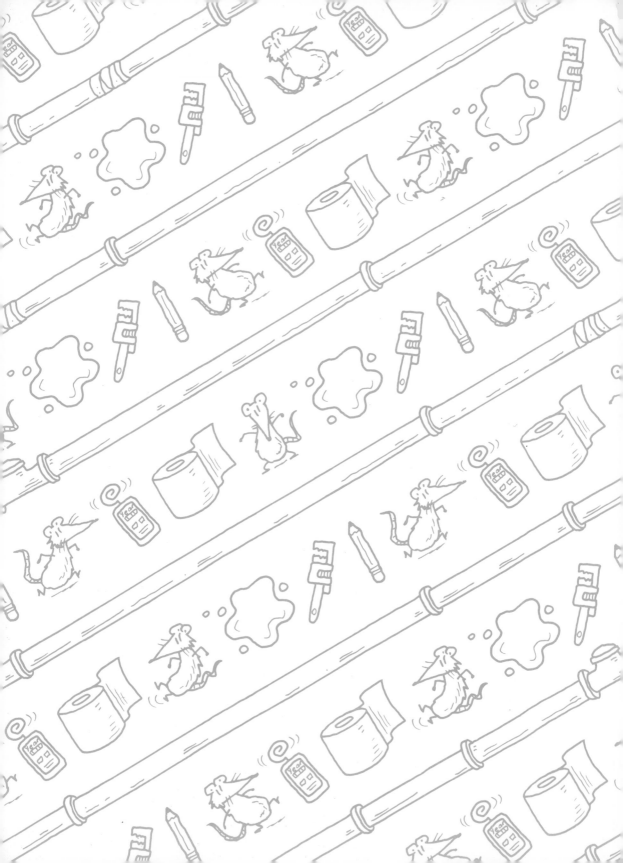